The Voice of a Master

GW00391407

It is Jesus Himself Who Speaks

Know Thyself

By Eileen McCourt

The Voice of a Master:

It is Jesus himself who speaks – know thyself
By Eileen McCourt

The Voice of a Master: It is Jesus himself who speaks – know thyself.

This book was first published in Great Britain in paperback during November 2018.

The moral right of Eileen McCourt is to be identified as the author of this work and has been asserted by her in accordance with the Copyright, Designs and Patents Act of 1988.

ISBN: 978- 1731330369

CONTENTS

ABOUT THE AUTHOR

Eileen McCourt is a retired school teacher of English and History with a Master's degree in History from University College Dublin.

She is also a Reiki Grand Master teacher and practitioner, having qualified in Ireland, England and Spain, and has introduced many of the newer modalities of Reiki healing energy into Ireland for the first time, from Spain and England. Eileen has qualified in England through the Lynda Bourne School of Enlightenment, and in Spain through the Spanish Federation of Reiki with Alessandra Rossin, Bienstar, Santa Eulalia, Ibiza.

Regular workshops and healing sessions are held in Elysium Wellness, Newry, County Down; New Moon Holistics N.I. Carrickfergus, County Antrim; Angel Times Limerick; Holistic Harmony Omagh, County Tyrone; Spirit 3 Ballinasloe, County Galway; Sacred Space Newbridge, County Kildare; Celtic School of Sound Healing, Swords, County Dublin and Flagmount Wild Garden, County Clare, where Eileen teaches all of the following to both practitioner and teacher levels:

- **Tibetan Usui Reiki levels 1, 2, 3 (Inner Master) 4 (teacher) and Grand Master**

- **Tera-Mai Reiki Seichem**

- **Okuna Reiki (Atlantean and Lemurian)**

- **Reiki Karuna (Indian)**

- **Rahanni Celestial Healing**

- **Fire Spirit Reiki (Christ Consciousness and Holy Spirit)**

- **Mother Mary Reiki**

- Mary Magdalene Reiki
- Archangels Reiki
- Archangel Ascended Master Reiki
- Reiki Seraphim
- Violet Flame Reiki
- Lemurian Crystal Reiki
- Golden Eagle Reiki (Native North American Indian)
- Golden Chalice Reiki
- Golden Rainbow Ray Reiki
- Goddesses of Light Reiki
- Unicorn Reiki
- Pegasus Reiki
- Elementals Reiki
- Dragon Reiki
- Dolphin Reiki
- Pyramid of Goddess Isis Reiki
- Kundalini Reiki
- Magnified Healing of the God Most High of the Universe
- Psychic Surgery
- Merkaba Activation and Meditation

Details of all of these modalities can be found on Eileen's website.

This is Eileen's **17th** book.

Previous publications include:

- **'Living the Magic'**, published in December 2014

- **'This Great Awakening'**, September 2015

- **'Spirit Calling! Are You Listening?'**, January 2016

- **'Working With Spirit: A World of Healing'**, January 2016

- **'Life's But A Game! Go With The Flow!'**, March 2016

- **'Rainbows, Angels and Unicorns!'**, April 2016

- **'........And That's The Gospel Truth!'**, September 2016

- **'The Almost Immaculate Deception! The Greatest Scam in History?'**, September 2016

- **'Are Ye Not Gods?' The true inner meanings of Jesus' teachings and messages'**, March 2017

- **'Jesus Lost and Found'**, July 2017

- **'Behind Every Great Man........ Mary Magdalene Twin Flame of Jesus'**, July 2017

- **'Out of the Mind and into the Heart: Our Spiritual Journey with Mary Magdalene'**, August 2017

- **'Divinely Designed: The Oneness of the Totality of ALL THAT IS'**, January 2018

- **'Resurrection or Resuscitation? What really happened in That Tomb?'**, May 2018

- **'Music of the Spheres: Connecting to the Great Universal Consciousness and to ALL THAT IS through the music of Irish** *composer /pianist Pat McCourt',* June 2018

- **'Chakras, Crystals, Colours and Drew the Dragon: A child's second Spiritual book',** July 2018

Eileen has also recorded 6 guided meditation CDs with her brother, pianist Pat McCourt:

- *'Celestial Healing'*

- *'Celestial Presence'*

- *'Cleansing, energising and balancing the Chakras'*

- *'Ethereal Spirit' - Meditation on the 'I Am Presence'*

- *'Open the Door to Archangel Michael'*

- *'Healing with Archangel Raphael'*

Eileen's first DVD, 'Living the Magic' has also been released, a live interview in which Eileen talks about matters Spiritual.

All publications are available from Amazon online and all publications and CDs are in Angel and Holistic centres around the country, as specified on website.

Website: www.celestialhealing8.co.uk

ACKNOWLEDGEMENTS

As always, I wish to thank my publishers, Don Hale OBE and Dr. Steve Green for their support, their guidance and advice, and above all for their patience! I call Steve 'Hawk Eye' as he spots and fixes everything, sometimes even before I have it written! To coin a phrase, Steve 'has my back' and urges me on when I get lazy. Thank you Steve!

And my sincere thanks, yet again, to my family and my wonderful friends for their constant support and encouragement. You all know who you are!

Sincere and heart-felt appreciation to all of you who are buying my books and CDs and for your kind comments. I am just happy that my books are helping you on your Spiritual path!

Thank you to all who attend my workshops and courses, and to all who have taken the time to write reviews for me, both in my books and on Amazon. You are greatly appreciated!

And as always, I give thanks for all the great blessings that are constantly being sent our way in this wonderful, loving, abundant universe.

Namaste!

Eileen McCourt

December 2018

NOTE TO READER

For the purpose of this book, I have used the esoteric teachings of Jesus as in the *'Gospel of Thomas'* and the *'Gospel of Mary of Magdala'.* The Gospel of Thomas was amongst those texts unearthed at Nag Hammadi in the upper desert region of Egypt in 1945. The Gospel of Mary of Magdala, written in the early second century C.E. came to light in Cairo in the late nineteenth century. Neither of these texts were included in the four canonical gospels of the Roman Christian Church.

In his last incarnation on this earth energy vibration frequency, Jesus was known by his Hebrew name, **Yeshua**, pronounced with the emphasis on the middle syllable (Yesh-**u**-a). Jesus is the Romanised version of that name and the name by which most people still recognise him. Yeshua is now recognised as **Ascended Master Sananda** in the higher energy vibration frequencies.

I have used both names, Jesus and Yeshua throughout this book, to remind the reader that the person most people still recognise as Jesus is referred to in all the Nag Hammadi texts by his Hebrew name, Yeshua.

I do wish to emphasise that this book is **NOT** a direct channelling from Jesus, but rather, I have used the esoteric teachings from the afore-mentioned texts to support the explanations and answers I have offered to some of life's most challenging questions.

REVIEWS

A wonderful new addition to Eileen McCourt's list of insightful reads. The Voice of a Master is a statement of what is, what was and what will always be. Eileen's explanation of our world and our human condition is scientific, in depth and hugely life-affirming. She speaks to the Soul. Eileen explains how the new sciences of quantum physics is rediscovering the ancient shamanic understanding of the fractal nature of the Universe and of time. That we are a small element of something so monumentally huge that we are both miniscule and yet so unbelievably all encompassing, all at the same time. Each one of us is a thread in the fabric of the Universe, in that, we are all one and we are God. The path of our Soul is not the one we have been conventionally told. Yet, McCourt draws from the understanding that was once in every community, in every culture around the world, that we are on a cyclical path of birth, death and rebirth, one of the great truths of the Universe, that matter does not die, it restructures and so do we. We are here for soul expansion, as our soul expands, so does our Universe and we are eternally linked to this process. Our soul path is as it is described on the stones at Newgrange, on a spiral path. Eileen explains how societal organisations have conspired to keep this essential information about ourselves, away from us, as a factor of power and control. But, no longer. The word is out and science is catching up and rediscovering these essential truths. Eileen's book is masterful, insightful and screams truth. We have forgotten our power and also the responsibility that comes with that. This is not new news, it is old wisdom and as a species we have forgotten the real essence of ourselves, our world and our purpose on this planet. Eileen has reminded us. A ground-breaking read!

Declan Quigley of Anam Nasca, Irish Shamanism.

Eileen McCourt successfully extrapolates the wisdom of Jesus' teachings to share with us the pathway to spiritual awareness and enlightenment. Eloquently yet simply written. 'The Voice of a Master: It is Jesus himself who speaks' gives us the keys to a more fulfilled and deserving way of life. Enjoy!

Clare Bowman, Spiritual Historian

FOREWORD

'Whoever has self-knowledge, the world cannot contain them.'

'Those who know the All, yet do not know themselves are deprived of everything.'

The words of the Master Jesus himself, as delivered to us in the Gospel of Thomas, one of the hidden texts found at Nag Hammadi in the desert in Upper Egypt in 1945.

These words are not just a figure of speech. They go deeper than that. Much deeper. *Self-knowledge* is all about knowing what and who each one of us truly is. It has nothing to do with the mind or what we ordinarily consider to be thought. Nor has it anything to do with understanding our personality, our likes and dislikes, or how we present ourselves to the world.

Self-knowledge is a consciousness, an awareness of the energy which each one of us is, and our connection to the countless other vibration energy frequencies which surround us on all sides, constantly inter-communicating, inter-penetrating, inter-being with us and with each other.

If we do not understand our basic inherent nature as a constantly changing form of energy, an energy consciousness, and all that entails, then we are not living life as we are meant to live it. We are not living life to our full potential, to our full magnificent, unlimited capacity.

If your car is not performing as it should do, then you get a qualified mechanic to fix it, and in order to fix it, that mechanic needs to understand how a car works.

It's the same with life! If you are not living in joy, harmony and inner peace, then something about your life needs fixing. And in order to fix what is wrong, then you need to understand the whole meaning to life, how it works and why we are here.

We are meant to live in joy, harmony and inner peace, it's our natural birthright. We are meant to enjoy life! By all accounts, Jesus certainly enjoyed a good party and socialising with his friends. And look at Buddha! Always smiling! Those iconic images of Jesus on the cross that we see everywhere in Christian churches and grave yards give us a picture of doom and gloom, certainly not the way in which Jesus himself would have wanted us to remember him!

And we need to take responsibility for our own life!

If I told you that those who read all, or even any of my books, will get a plenary indulgence, which in Church terms means, as some have been taught, that their time in purgatory will be reduced and they will be admitted into heaven sooner, or, as others have been taught, that their sins are completely forgiven and they now start with a clean slate, would you believe me? Conversely, if I told you that those who do not read my books will burn in the flames of hell for all eternity, would you believe me?

Ridiculous, daft and preposterous as these claims would be, they are no more ridiculous or any more daft or preposterous than many of the other claims that a great number of people living on this earth believe are true, and in which they have placed their utmost trust and faith to get them into heaven.

Caught up in a world which appears to many people to offer mostly uncertainty, depression, fear, suffering, ruthless competition, survival of only the fittest, scarcity and want, loss and despair, how is it at all possible to even just survive, never mind find that elusive joy, happiness and peace which some seemingly lucky, fortunate people constantly exude and which the seemingly unlucky, unfortunate all others seem to spend their lives chasing after but never find?

We have been programmed to believe that this world is all against us, that we have been thrown into the surging ocean of life without even a life-belt, destined to struggle on as best we can through one stormy crisis after another. And in the end, all we do is die anyway! Then we have to face that terrible judgement, condemned for all eternity for the mess we made of everything, despite the fact that all the odds were stacked against us from the very beginning! Unfair or what?

And we have been further programmed to believe that we are sinners, worthless, not good enough. No wonder we live in a state of unhappiness and discontent! Waiting to be judged and punished by an obscure God who remains faceless and hidden, whose standards are so high that we will never match up, and whose judgement and subsequent condemnation remains non-negotiable, cemented in concrete, indelibly inked in the great book of records, which of course, is stored in heaven.

Just as a struggling, drowning swimmer will clutch at anything to save himself, so too we have been clutching desperately at whatever and whoever promises us they will save us. This has been the story right down through history. Join our club, pay your money, follow our rules and you will be saved! We will save you! A very attractive package! And what do we do? We clutch at the straw!

But the time has finally come! The time when most people are ready for much more than such flimsy promises from such flimsy institutions as controlling religions can possibly offer them. The time has come for wakening up! The time when people are asking questions, those same questions, which if asked in previous centuries, would have resulted in accusations of heresy and the punishment of torture and death for such a crime. Let us not forget how those who first discovered and taught that the earth is round or that the earth revolves around the sun, were condemned as heretics and persecuted by the Roman Christian Church! Simply because they dared to contradict Church teachings! And even though those teachings turned out to be wrong! Those days are gone. Gone for good. Returning no more! Buried beneath the shifting sands, lost behind the thickening mists of time!

It was the twentieth century Swiss psychiatrist, psychoanalyst and founder of analytical psychology, Carl Gustav Jung who wrote, '*Your vision will become clear only when you can look into your heart. Who looks outside, dreams; who looks inside, awakens.*'

Yes! There is indeed a wonderful great awakening happening all over the world! More and more people are stirring out of their slumber, stirring from life-times of repression and deceit, and in seeking Spiritual growth, no longer looking to external forces or self-proclaimed powers and authorities to guide them through life, but instead connecting with the inherent divinity each one of us is, and the power each one of us possesses, raising our Spiritual consciousness beyond this physicality of our earth dimension. People are now increasingly more able and willing to look beyond, and expand their thinking beyond the physical situations in life and so awaken to what and who we all really are, expanding far beyond these physical limitations.

'*Whoever has self-knowledge the world cannot contain them.*'

Knowing our inherent nature, who and what we are, puts us beyond anything this world can throw at us, beyond being affected by worldly matters, beyond concerning ourselves unnecessarily with the trivial matters that concern us on a daily basis.

There is no doubt we are now living in extraordinary times. Extraordinary in the sense that all the structures which we thought were holding society together and in which we placed our trust, because they did, after all, promise us everything and told us everything we wanted to hear, are tumbling and crumbling all around us. And that is simply because those same structures, in which we placed our trust, were not holding us together at all in the first place! Those same structures that were founded on the lust for power, control and wealth, those at the top, in the higher echelons of society, right at the very top of the hierarchal edifice, manipulating the rest of us through the double-edged sword of fear and guilt. Paper-thin structures, unable to withstand the powerful, forceful, unstoppable winds of change and truth that are now blowing all around us.

As we progress along our path in what we see as linear time, and as we are exposed to more and more 'new' ideas, there is no doubt that science is now confirming what the ancient masters taught a long, long time ago. There are no 'new' ideas! These same ideas have been presented to us for aeons of time. We were just not listening. We were just not yet ready to listen. Breakthroughs in science, quantum physics and metaphysics confirm that there is no separation or 'going it alone', even on this earth dimension, where the rat race means that only the most competitive, only the most ruthless, only the most ambitious survive, the rest relegated to the periphery of society, castigated as losers, misfits, failures.

Life is not meant to be like this! Life is a game, not meant to be taken seriously, and in order to play we need to know the rules! We are meant to live in enjoyment, harmony, peace, trust and love.

We are meant to smell the roses! To smell the coffee! To enjoy the ride! To engage with the world, yes, but not to be completely immersed in it!

And the reason we are failing is because we have lost sight of so many important and vital basic principles. We have lost touch with our own essential nature! Our own Divine Essence! We are lacking in *self-knowledge*!

What each of us really is, a Spiritual being having a physical experience for the duration of each and every lifetime for which we willingly and freely sign up, has absolutely nothing to do with our physical body or our brain. The reality of each and every one of us is that we are immortal. That means that the energy of which we are composed, the energy which we all are, will never end, it will never die. We will never die. Our physical body is just that, physical, and therefore subject to all the laws governing matter and mass. That means that like all matter, like all mass, it will decay and corrupt.

Great Spiritual masters and teachers of humanity such as Buddha and Jesus, known as Yeshua, attempted to teach us the importance of knowing what and who we truly are. Their teachings remain as relevant today as they were over 2000 years ago. But those teachings have been thwarted and manipulated by those who used them for ulterior motives, seeking power and control.

I kid you not when I point out the fact that no Church or no government has ever, throughout the entire history of mankind, ever based its ethos or teachings on the words of Jesus! Seriously! No kidding!

So what is this book about? And how does this book differ from my previous books?

This book is a natural progression from my previous books in that it goes deeper into Spiritual matters, deeper and further towards *knowing the self.* And in *knowing the self*, each one of us is able to live life to our full potential, able to replace the negativity and lack of hope we see all around us in these so-called modern times, with positivity and hope which come from knowing the truth, understanding who and what we truly are. And that understanding is key to us finding inner peace, happiness and joy, enabling us to live a peaceful, tranquil life, exuding that joy and happiness, undisturbed and unruffled by the constant turmoil going on all around us. In other words, how to retain your inner peace and tranquility when all around you are losing theirs.

The key to achieving happiness, peace, tranquility and fulfilment during this and every life time lies in accepting that we are Spiritual beings, and not just mere physical beings. And when we accept this, we will pay more attention to our Spiritual body than we are currently paying to our physical body, because the Spiritual body is the real us, the physical body is not the real us, being as it is, impermanent, transitory, and subject to decay. That's it in a nutshell!

So allow yourself to get in touch with the real you, the energy consciousness, the beautiful Spiritual light you truly are! I am not telling you to ignore the physical you! That would indeed be fool-hardy! I am merely putting things into perspective. And it's all about perspective!

Perspective! Perspective! Perspective!

The sole reason for us being here on this earth plane in the first place is to further our soul evolution! We are not here to gather as much material possessions, wealth, titles, as we possibly can in the short space of time allotted to us! Unfortunately, that is where humanity has taken the wrong path! Pursuit of happiness through material possessions, wealth, power, control, does not bring what we are looking for! Those are all transitory, just like our physical body!

And yes! We can live a life of happiness, joy, peace, tranquility and fulfilment while in a physical body! The Master Jesus has told us how! '*Know thyself* '!

It was indeed Yeshua the Nazarene, Yeshua the Essene, known to us as Jesus, who taught us just how to do that, 2000 years ago. But the Jesus we know about from the four specially-doctored canonical gospels did not exist! The Jesus of those gospels was a composite figure, thought up as an expediency, to bolster up the new Roman Christian Church, a figure manufactured to spear-head the new religion of the Roman Empire and cement that straggling Roman Empire under the one banner of Christianity, a Christianity based, not on the teachings of Jesus, but on all the old superstitious beliefs of the Roman and Greek gods with whom people of that time would have been so familiar, and which Yeshua the Essene tried to change.

The teachings of Yeshua the Essene are what we need to look at in order to find out how we can achieve *self-knowledge*, and so live life to our full potential.

Yeshua did not come to found a new religion or a new Church. Rather, he was trying to change people's attitudes and beliefs about the world and life. Trying to show us who and what we truly are. Trying to direct us towards *self-knowledge*, towards '*Knowing thyself'.*

You are in control of your own life! Fact! You and you alone have the power to decide whether you want to trundle through life, moaning and groaning in your victim-poor-me mentality, in your limited belief that you are just a physical body, or whether you live your life in joy, harmony and inner peace, in the limitless *self-knowledge* of who and what you truly are. Who in their right mind would choose the former when they can have the latter?

*'**Know thyself!**'* Knowing yourself means simply knowing the whole you. Not just the physical you, but the whole you. And when we know and understand the whole of who and what we truly are, then we can indeed smell those roses, we can indeed smell that coffee, and we can indeed start to enjoy this great roller-coaster ride we call life!

So come with me through the pages of this book and discover the whole you, and in discovering the whole you, in discovering you in your limitless entirety, you will indeed come to '***know thyself**'.

And in ***knowing thyself***, gaining ***self-knowledge***, you will become an awakened human being, you will experience joy and freedom, freedom from restrictive and controlling external forces, allowing your immortal soul to fly freely as it should, singing its own glorious song in the magnificence of the Great Universal Consciousness, the Great Universal Energy, the Great Collective Energy Field we call God.

Namaste!

CHAPTER 1:

Fact of the Matter - What we are

You are much more than you think you are or believe yourself to be.

You are not just a particular shade of flesh covering a mass of neatly arranged bones, parading around and disguised as a mechanical something, wired up to respond to impulses emitting from a command-issuing centralised brain.

And you are most certainly not an evolutionary accident or freak mishap, a random or arbitrary configuration of cells, germs or genes, a selection of something out of a lucky-dip scenario, struggling just to survive, as Charles Darwin would have you believe.

Neither are you any sort of chemical equation or chemical reaction.

And as for what the seventeenth century French philosopher Rene Descartes would have you believe, that your mind is separate from your body, '*Cogito, ergo sum*' (I think, therefore I am), well, that does not do you justice either!

Nor are you what the late seventeenth century Isaac Newton, known as the founder of modern physics, suggested you are - a machine, operating within the greater machine of the universe, where everything follows certain set laws of motion. A sort of robot, automatically caught up in an uncontrollable pre-destined chain of events. Far from it!

These earlier century theories formed an established base of scientific thinking up until recent times. As we move along, however, in what we see as linear time, new ideas replace old ones. New ideas are always considered heretical and opposed as detrimental to the established way of thinking. And the world of scientific thinking has always been considered very conservative. Many new scientific discoveries are still being suppressed and ignored. If a new discovery suggests that modern science has got something wrong, or not exactly correct, then that new discovery is denied, ridiculed, suppressed.

They laughed at Copernicus and Galileo and the Christian Church suppressed them. They laughed at the Wright brothers too. In fact, history shows a long list of scientific discoveries which were ridiculed as bizarre at first, treated with genuine hostile prejudice and discarded, only to be later accepted. Probably the best known example of just such a scenario was the theory that the world was flat, the exact same world later proven to be round. And of course, Galileo's theory that the earth revolves around the sun, contradicting the previous belief that the sun moved around the earth.

But, as Victor Hugo, nineteenth century French poet, dramatist and novelist, creator of '*The Hunchback of Notre Dame*' said, '*All the forces in the world are not as powerful as an idea whose time has come.*'

And the nineteenth century Polish philosopher, Schopenhauer, wrote in respect of the evolving stages of truth: '*First, it is ridiculed, second it is violently opposed, and third, it is accepted as being self-evident.'*

We have the science of physics and we have metaphysics. What is the difference? While physics is all about nature, natural phenomenon, matter, motion, energy, space, time, and our understanding of all relationships between things, metaphysics, on the other hand, is a division of philosophy that deals with the fundamental nature of reality and being. As such, it tries to answer much deeper questions beyond our physical vision and scope, such as why we or the universe exist, the nature of man and our place in creation. Metaphysics, while not being any sort of religion, deals more with the Spiritual than the physical. The great metaphysical poets, such as the sixteenth century John Donne, have all attempted to go beyond what we see and feel with our physical body and throw light on what is happening all around us, but to which we are not tuned in. Indeed, the metaphysics of today may well become the physics of tomorrow.

And we now have quantum physics! Quantum physics being the theoretical basis of modern physics that explains the nature and behaviour of matter and energy on the atomic and subatomic level, as forwarded by Max Planck, a German theoretical physicist, considered to be the initial founder of quantum theory, and one of the most important physicists of the 20th Century.

So how does quantum physics differ from classical physics?

Quantum physics, like metaphysics, makes use of aesthetic arguments when establishing theories. In classical physics, particle behaviour is seen through the naked eye, for example Newton's laws of motion, and particles move in orderly, predictable and smooth patterns. In quantum physics, on the other hand, particle behaviour is considered at microscopic level, with particles behaving both as particles and as waves, and in an unpredictable manner, as forwarded by Werner Karl Heisenberg in his Heisenberg Theory of Uncertainty. Heisenberg was another 20th Century German theoretical physicist, another key pioneer of quantum mechanics, publishing his work in 1925 in a break-through paper.

Quantum physics is divided into Newtonian and relativistic physics, where everything exists relative to everything else. Quantum physics, on the other hand, is subdivided into varying levels of statistical probabilities and wave lengths.

Physics itself has now been overtaken by quantum physics. Where we once had household names like Aristotle, Isaac Newton, Darwin, Descartes, even Albert Einstein, we now have such names as Max Planck, Louis de Broglie, Werner Heisenberg, Hal Puthoff, Fritz Albert Popp, Denis Gabor, Walter Schempp, William Braud, Kepler, Schrodinger, Morley, to mention but a few. These pioneers have and are changing the whole way we look at our world, the universe and entire creation. Current thinking is indeed far removed from that of the seventeenth century.

Where the science of physics, as we know it to be, has its limitations, explaining various phenomena occurring in the universe only upon the basis of Newtonian laws and principles, quantum physics and metaphysics on the other hand, have no limitations. For example, when the waves crash on the shore, they make a certain sound. But if there is no-one on the shore to hear them crashing, do they still make a sound? If so, then sounds are occurring all the time beyond our knowledge and awareness. So physics is restricted in the sense that it can only explain things that can be observed or heard while quantum physics shows that an object can be both wave, (i.e. energy) and particle, (i.e. matter), both present and absent at the same time. And the existence of something is totally independent of our actual physical hearing it or seeing it.

And here is where metaphysics and quantum physics come in. They are both actually a continuum of physics in that they go beyond what is observable and quantifiable. They deal with the whole of reality, the infinite reality, the intelligible reality, and the Spiritual reality. While physics brings us to the edge of the universe, it is metaphysics and quantum physics that bring us beyond those boundaries, to our being and knowing, beyond what we can see with our five physical senses. Modern physics is no longer just Newtonian physics, but has advanced to quantum physics.

And metaphysics and quantum physics have given us a whole new understanding of what and who we really are and our place in the entirety of creation.

'Sure I'm only human' as we all often say when trying to excuse ourselves for what we see as some short-fall or failing on our part, comes nowhere near defining what or who each one of us really is.

We now know there are dimensions to our being, hidden depths of consciousness of which we appear to be as yet totally unaware. And we know that we are surrounded by numerous other subtle fields of energy, all interpenetrating our physical body, constantly interacting with us and with each other.

The ancient Shamans knew about and understood these non-physical dimensions and energy vibrations all around us, as did our ancestors. For them, there was no duality or separateness. We, however, have separated our physicality from the rest of life, and the result is that we exist merely in our body and mind, apart from and outside of the world of Spirit and energy, and not an inherent part of that world, as we should be. You cannot live through your mind. Your mind is not who you are! Your mind is only a tool. That's all! And so, most people experience only about ten percent of reality! Most people are living only about ten percent of what they should be living and experiencing! Way below par! We limit ourselves severely by living our lives merely through our mind, thoughts, actions and feelings, and through our very limited five physical senses. But that's not who or what we are! You are not your thoughts. You are not your feelings. You are not your emotions.

So to repeat, you are not just your physical body! You cannot be just that!

Consider this! You can change your physical body in numerous ways. You can have a complete body make-over. You can have cosmetic surgery to give your body a completely new shape. You can have a heart or other organ transplant, or hip or knee replacements, or have tattoos here there and everywhere on your body. But no matter what you do to your body, you are still you! So there obviously must be more to you than just your physical body!

And there is obviously a lot more to our existence here in this world than we are at present allowing ourselves to experience!

In the Gospel of Thomas we read:

'If you do not fast from the world, you will not find the Kingdom.'

The reality is that each one of us is a unique manifestation, a unique expression of Source energy, a stream of consciousness, in continuous motion, ongoing, pure potential playing in a field of infinite possibility! And that's certainly a lot more than just a physical body can offer!

Most of us are unable to fix our own car, washing machine or any other electrical gadget simply because we do not understand how the whole machine works. In order to fix what is wrong with the car or what is not working as it is meant to do, we need to understand how the car works. Not understanding how a car works however, does not mean we cannot enjoy driving it. Nor do we need to know about the inside workings of a watch in order to get the required use from it. But, if we do understand something about the workings of any particular commodity, machine or gadget, then we can certainly benefit greatly by easing and enhancing our experience. Probably even prolong its life! For example, if we know that the car needs oil, water and tyres checked every so often, as well as serviced by a qualified mechanic, then we can certainly enhance our experience of driving the car, because it will perform better for us!

It is the same with life!

In order to have an enhanced life, living in enjoyment, happiness, trust, peace and contentment, we need to understand how life works. We need to understand what we are and why we are here on this earth plane. We need to understand the numerous subtle energies that surround us and of which we ourselves are composed. Otherwise, we just stagger and wobble along, at the mercy of wind and rain, lurching from one drama to another, tossed about by storm after storm, clinging on with our finger nails, paralyzed with fear and unable to enjoy any part of the exhilarating ride. We need to understand our essential basic nature and essence.

Everything is energy. Absolutely everything. Everything that is either visible or invisible to us in our surroundings is made or composed of energy. And that includes us. Energy is the building block, the basic, vital ingredient, the main, staple constituent of entire Creation.

And what is energy? Energy is consciousness. Consciousness is life. Life is consciousness. It's all energy!

And energy and awareness or consciousness of life is constantly changing, taking different forms and shapes, but never ending. Energy never dies. It cannot be killed off. So each one of us, as a form of energy, as a particular level of consciousness, will never end, we will merely change our form of energy, our level of consciousness. Like the energy, the consciousness of the brook, in the poem of the same title by Alfred Lord Tennyson, *'I go on forever'*.

The consciousness of any and every living thing is the basic premise, the core, the fundamental base from which it operates. It

8

is the level of awareness which each living entity experiences at any given time. Awareness of what? Awareness of our very being. Awareness of the Oneness in which we all exist. And awareness of the fact that we are part of a greater whole. So should *'I think, therefore I am'* not read instead *'I am, therefore I think'* ?

Energy operates on different energy frequency vibration levels. We have all been taught in our science classes in school that everything in this world, ourselves included, is composed of matter,- such things as atoms, molecules, photons, protons, electrons, etc.

And what is the relationship between matter and energy? We have just seen that energy is the core of everything. And that includes matter. So matter is inherent in energy, like everything else.

$E = mc^2$. E= m multiplied by c^2. Albert Einstein's famous theory of relativity, the theory that established the relationship between matter, or mass, and energy.

The E in the equation stands for Energy. The m stands for mass and the c stands for the speed of Light, the rate at which Light travels. So, the full interpretation of the equation is that energy equals or manifests itself as mass or matter, which is any object or thing, ourselves included, moving at various speeds, from slow to very high speed, specifically the speed of light squared.

In other words, in its simplified form, mass or any physical thing that we can see, is just energy slowed down. Energy slowed down to a rate of speed where it can be identified as a particular object or being.

So matter, or mass, mass being just another name for matter, and which is what we in our physical bodies are, is simply energy vibrating more slowly than the energy vibrating in the various Spiritual levels. This earth dimension, this earth plane is the most dense of all the energy vibration frequencies. The energy of which we are composed is slowed right down for us to be able to identify each other, as solid matter, and to keep us on this earth plane. *The fact of the matter! That's us!*

Consider this. When you watch the propeller of a plane or helicopter spinning round, you just see a blur. Or when you watch even a fast bicycle, you cannot see the spokes in the wheels because it is travelling so fast, but if it slows down until it has practically stopped, you can make out every detail. Or your washing machine. When the drum is going round at full speed, you cannot identify any of the clothes inside because of the high speed at which it is revolving. But when it slows down or stops, you can clearly identify each particular piece of clothing. Or indeed, a child's toy spinning top. The faster it spins, the more it becomes a spinning sphere, completely losing its original shape.

So, when energy exists and moves at very high speed or what we call high vibrations, we cannot see it. But when it slows down, and as it is in the process of slowing down, it starts gathering molecules, becoming mass and manifesting as a solid thing, which we can see and identify.

The only difference between all the forms of energy is the vibrational frequency at which each form operates, the different level of consciousness each experiences. Just like all the television or radio channels! When you are tuned into one particular frequency, watching one particular programme on that particular channel, all the other channels are not gone off somewhere else. They are still around, in the system, but not visible to you because you are not tuned into them.

There are countless energy vibration frequencies and dimensions all around us, all inter-connecting, inter-playing, inter-exchanging all the time, and all on different levels of lightness and purity. As we have just seen, most people cannot see these forms of energy around them because of the high vibrational speed at which the energy is travelling, making it invisible to the human eye. Mediums, psychics and highly Spiritually evolved people can often see energy though, because they are able to tune into other frequency levels, simply because their own frequency level is high enough to enable them to do so. Other people can feel or sense the presence of some other energy around them.

We have just seen that energy is at the same time a wave (energy) and a particle (matter). So we are both energy and matter. We as human beings, physical beings, are just energy slowed right down and manifesting as solid physical matter. The matter part of us is our physical body. This vibrates on a slow frequency level, so we can see it. The energy part of us is our energy body, our soul, our Spirit. This vibrates on a high level, a fast speed, and so we cannot see it.

Most people are aware that they have a body and a soul. But not everyone understands what this entails.

So what is the difference between our physical body and our soul, which is our energy body?

We **have** a physical body. But we **are** a soul, we **are** an energy body. That's the difference! Our physical body is contained within our energy or Spiritual body, and not the other way about, as many people think. No surgeon, while performing an operation has ever found a soul inside a human body!

I have just explained why we cannot see our energy body, - because it is on a high vibration frequency, moving at a greater speed than our physical mass body, which is on a much more dense, slow vibration frequency. But this was not always the case!

Our ancient ancestors were very aware of their energy or Spirit body. Artists and painters down through the centuries have depicted fields of light, a luminous radiance, a soft emanation of light, around human bodies, in particular the halo around the head area. All the great Eastern religions have done likewise. And halos around people have even been found in pre-historic cave paintings.

So what has happened that we no longer are able to see all of this?

The answer is that we have numbed and dulled our senses to being open to it all. The rise of industrialization and the incumbent growth of urbanization with all that these entail have deprived us of our inherent ability to see or sense other forms of energy around us. Furthermore, modern day views are mostly rational and logical, and science has steered us to depend only on our five physical senses for the evidence of anything being in existence or not.

With the current shift in our earth's energy, however, more and more people are returning to being aware again of their own energy body and the other energies constantly surrounding us. More and more people are awakening to the ***facts of the matter.***

We are first and foremost Spiritual beings, Spiritual beings having a physical experience for the duration of this life-time. We have experienced many previous life-times and we will no doubt experience many more. Eternity is not something which just starts after we pass over or transition back to Spirit. This is eternity, the here and now, and this present life-time is just one of our many walk-abouts across the vastness of infinity, across the fathomless expanse of eternity. We are all Spiritual travellers, inter-galactic nomads, multi and inter-dimensional beings, journeying throughout the entire cosmos, traversing the infinity of creation, transcending time and space through different vibrational frequencies, in differing levels of reality.

There are 7 main energetic dimension levels, dimensions of reality, each level divided into countless further levels. Starting with the first, the dimension that includes rocks and other substances with limited consciousness, and which do not procreate, they progress upwards to the highest dimension, the seventh dimension, where there is total integration and where there is no form, only pure light, only pure consciousness.

In between the highest and the lowest, plants and animals exist on the second dimension, with a consciousness and a biological identity, and also the ability to procreate. We humans exist on the third and fourth dimensions, having a physicality and also a consciousness. Here on the third dimension, and only on this third dimension, we experience space as empty, and time as lineal. In the fourth dimension, we have a greater awareness of community, collectiveness and Oneness. We experience empathy and telepathy, and we experience time as cyclical and in a spiral. And as we progress upwards through the higher levels of the fourth dimension, we begin to recall our past lives and recognise those around us with whom we have shared past lives.

Spiritual guides, Ascended Masters, and high energy frequency beings of Light reside in the fifth dimension, where the veil has been lifted, and there is clear recall of everything.

In the sixth dimension dwell the likes of Buddha and Jesus, and all those who have already achieved Enlightenment and have arrived back with Source. This is the Christ Consciousness dimension, the highest energy frequency within the entire Universal God Consciousness, from where the mature soul can manifest in other dimensions.

It is towards the seventh dimension, total immersion with the Universal God Energy that we are all heading, but most of us have a long, long way to go! Simply because most people are still very limited in soul consciousness and soul awareness. And before you ask, why are the likes of Buddha and Jesus not in the seventh dimension? Simply because they have freely chosen to remain in the sixth dimension, helping humanity until all of humanity has ascended.

SOUL AND HIGHER SELF

Our soul, our divine Spirit, our energy body, is immortal. It will never die or cease to be. Our body, on the other hand, is merely the casing, the wrapping, the outward visible layer through which we present ourselves to the world, and through which most people recognise us and see us to be. Just as we discard an old, worn-out coat when we have no further need for it or when it has outlived its present usefulness, so too, the physical body in which we have our soul encased for the duration of this life-time, we will also discard. It has served its present purpose. We no longer need it. We are in the process of transitioning back to Spirit, from whence we have all come, and we have no further need of a physical body. Our soul disconnects from our physical body at the point of transition, with our last breath, and expands outwards along a silver cord. When that silver cord snaps or disconnects, that silver cord that connects our body to our soul, then that is the point of no return for us back into our physical body. We are on our way home! Again! Back to the Light from whence we came!

And what exactly is our soul? Our soul is that over-riding totality of what and who we are, what we have ever been and what we ever will be. Each time we reincarnate on this earth plane, we do not need to take all of our soul with us, only the small percentage that we actually need for this time around. For example, we do not need to take with us all we have ever been in every other life-time. The greater portion of our soul remains in the higher vibrational frequencies, and this is our *Higher Self*, us in our undiluted, pure Divine God Essence. And when we pray, it is with this, our own inherent God Essence with which we are connecting, and it is from this same Higher Self we get the guidance that we need. Herein is the meaning of God. God is not some external force outside of ourselves, who grants some requests and refuses others, as we have been brought up to believe.

'Are ye not Gods?' The words of the Master Yeshua himself!

As we will see again later, God is not some external remote figure outside of ourselves. We ourselves **ARE** the God essence. This is not some sort of Spiritual arrogance or blasphemy! It is just us reclaiming our natural Divine Essence. So why do we continue to search for God when we already are that for which we are searching?

I am sure you are familiar with the phrase *'God helps those who help themselves!'*

Just another way of saying *'self-service!'*

THE AURA

Our physical body is surrounded on all sides by an energy field called our aura. Every form of life has its own aura attached to it. Plants, trees, flowers, animals, people, all are surrounded by a three-dimensional electro-magnetic energy field, and in the case of the human body, this takes an oval shape like an egg. Every organ, bone, limb, tissue, etc. has an energetic structure around it, holding and permeating it.

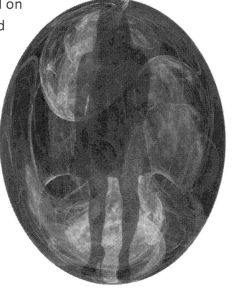

Our human energy body is composed of four layers, all extending outwards from the physical body, from the spine. The layer nearest to the physical body is called the etheric or the physical; next is the emotional; then the mental and finally the Spiritual. The first energy layer, the etheric or physical, is the most dense layer, the closest to the physical body, and is directly related to our general health and the physical functions of our human body. Because all the four layers extend outwards from the spine and overlap, this first layer, the etheric or physical, therefore contains all the other three layers as well. The second layer of energy surrounding us on all sides is the emotional energy layer, which obviously processes our emotions as we respond to events as they happen in our life. The third layer is the mental energy level, which stores all our

mental images and thought patterns.
The fourth layer is our Spiritual
energy layer, connecting us to our
Spiritual journey, our Spiritual
dimension. All these layers
interpenetrate and inter-connect
with each other. Because of this,
any event in your life affects, to
a greater or lesser extent, each
and every one of these layers. I
am sure you have heard of the
phantom limb sensation, where
even when the limb has been
removed, sensation, like itching, can
be felt, as if the limb is still there.

Consider this. You get stung by a wasp. Immediately your four
energy layers respond to what has just affected you. Your physical
energy layer registers the physical pain you are feeling in the
particular area of the sting. Your emotional energy layer initiates a
fear of wasps in you from now on. Your mental energy layer now
makes you think that wasps are always dangerous. And your
Spiritual energy layer may perhaps initiate you into thinking that
life itself is dangerous, and this begins to block the flow of
Universal Divine Energy to you.

So you can see how every event or happening in our life affects
each and every one of our four energy layers. Simply because they
are all over-lapping, inter-penetrating and inter-connecting. The
further from the physical body we get, our energy becomes less

visible, because it is getting further and further from the dense energy of the physical body.

So let us now look deeper at how these four energy layers are all inter-related, inter- connecting and over-lapping.

The first energy layer, the etheric or physical energy layer, as it is the closest to the physical body, contains all the other three energy layers as well, as they all permeate from the spine through it. The second energy layer, the emotional energy layer extends out further than the first layer, overlapping it. The third energy layer, the mental energy layer, extends out further from the spine than both the first and second energy layers, thus overlapping and inter-penetrating them both. Finally, the Spiritual energy layer, extending out the furthest from the spine, overlaps and inter-penetrates the other three energy layers. However, as this is the furthest energy layer extending from the spine, it is open on one side, as there is no other energy overlapping it on that side. This is the energy layer that connects us to all things Spiritual, extending out into infinity, beyond time and space, giving us the bigger picture of All That Is.

Our aura is constantly changing, depending on the thoughts we are sending out, the emotions we are feeling at any one time, the physical condition of our body, and is constantly interacting with the auric fields of others around us. No two of our auras are the same, and that is why when a Reiki or other holistic treatment is given, no two of us experience the same. The divine energy with which the practitioner is connecting, is of course the same for each of us, but when that divine energy connects with all our individual and unique auras, then it obviously produces a different effect for each one of us.

Every thought, every emotion, every feeling, all go outwards into our aura. Notice how, when you meet someone, you connect with them in either a positive way or in a negative way. Some people give you an instant lift, boosting your energy, while others drag you down, leaving you depleted and wondering what just happened. An energy vampire! That's what just happened! A hungry, prowling vampire looking for a feed, a fix! And you just happened to come along! Divine timing or what!

And what we send out through our aura attracts the same back to us. That's the irrefutable, the indisputable, the inviolable law of the universe, - like attracts like! A clear, clean high vibration aura attracts other clear, clean high vibration auras. Conversely, a dark, weak, lower vibration aura magnetises other dark, weak, lower vibration auras. There is an anomaly here however! Whilst dark auras attract only dark auras, bright clean auras on the other hand, whilst magnetising other clean bright auras to them, also fall prey to dark auras. And why? Because dark auras are looking for their energy fix! Energy vampires! And then along you come, your aura shining brightly! Of course they have you spotted! Like moths to a flame, like bees to the honey pot, they have registered you on their radar!

And just as our aura interconnects with the auras of others, so too, the auras of plants, flowers, trees and in fact everything in nature, interconnects with each other. And yes, they interconnect with us as well! Constantly! That's why spending time in nature is so therapeutic for us.

When Yeshua was healing people, he was not looking at the physical body, but beyond, into the aura. For Yeshua, it was as if the physical body did not even exist. It was the Spiritual body of each person with which he was connecting. He was reading the aura! And in reading the aura, he was able to read the physical condition of each particular person. That was simply because any illness or pain we suffer begins, not in our physical body, but in one or other of the outlying energy layers surrounding us. It just manifests in the physical body, the body of matter. So a holistic practitioner, unlike most medical practitioners, treats the whole body, physical, emotional, mental and Spiritual, as all these energy layers work as one.

You have all heard of the phrase, 'my own space'. That is simply the space around your physical body occupied by your aura, and if anyone is in too close proximity to you, you feel invaded. You feel their presence invading your privacy, as they are in your aura. You may well even feel intimidated or threatened, because when two auras are too near each other for comfort, they exchange information and inter-act with each other.

When you are with friends or family, you may of course feel very comfortable with a person being very near to your physical body. But you no doubt have noticed that at business meetings or political party meetings, often there is just a little distance between everyone as they sit around the table. In fact they sometimes seem to be squeezed in! This allows them to pick up on each other's thoughts! Conversely, at a game of cards or chess, the opponents usually sit across the table from each other, so that their thoughts cannot be picked up!

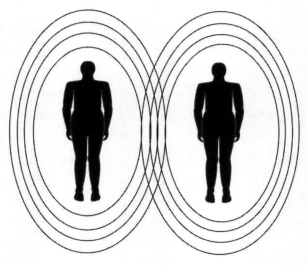

Our aura, our energy body, is often referred to as 'the human energy field'. It is the connecting force between our physical body and the Great Universal Energy Field or Universal Source. It is like a body map which others can read, telling everything about us, as it reflects our physical health, our thoughts and feelings.

And just as we need to keep our physical body clean and healthy, so too with our energy body. Here are a few meditation exercises to help you do just that.

TO CLEANSE AND RE-ENERGISE YOUR AURA

THE RAINBOW SHOWER

- Sit quietly. Close your eyes. Relax your body. Concentrate on your breathing.

- Imagine a shower of clear water pouring over you, cleansing all the negativity from your aura as it flows down over your body.

- Watch the murky water at your feet, as it washes away all the debris.

- Continue to watch as the murky water becomes clearer and clearer, as your aura is cleared of any darkness or shadows.

- Now imagine a shower of rainbow colours, pouring down over you, filling your aura with light and brightness, refreshing and energising you. Feel the colours of the rainbow touch every part of your body. Sink into the beauty of the rainbow colours for as long as you wish.

- Open your eyes, feeling refreshed and energised.

Eileen McCourt

CLEANSING AND RE-ENERGISING YOUR AURA

WITH ARCHANGEL MICHAEL

- Sit quietly. Close your eyes. Relax your body.

- Call on Archangel Michael to be present with you.

- Ask Archangel Michael to hoover up any darkness in your aura. Sense Archangel Michael's hoover moving around you, sucking up any negativity or auric debris.

- Now ask Michael to turn on the Light switch and fill the vacuum left in your aura with the healing White Light of the Holy Spirit.

- When you are ready, thank Archangel Michael.

- Open your eyes, feeling refreshed and energised.

PROTECTING YOUR ENERGY FIELD

PREVENTING YOUR ENERGY BEING DEPLETED BY OTHERS

- Sit quietly. Close your eyes. Relax your body.

- Cross your ankles, preventing the flow of energy out through your body.

- Join the tip of your thumb to the tip of your first finger, forming a circle, closing your energy circuit.

- You could also join the tip of your thumb to the tips of all your four fingers, forming a cone shape, closing your energy circuit.

- This exercise is very beneficial when you feel yourself being drained of energy by other people, or in any place where you feel the energy is draining and heavy.

GROUNDING YOURSELF

- Sit quietly. Close your eyes. Relax your body, your two feet firmly on the ground.

- Imagine roots, like tree roots growing from your feet right down into the earth, holding you firmly, keeping you secure, reaching right down into the soil, as far as you can go.

- Feel the connection with Mother Earth. Like the trees, you can sway and bend, but you can't fall over. You are securely grounded in Mother Earth.

When you are ready, thank Mother Earth for supporting you, and open your eyes.

PROTECTING YOURSELF

Every morning, say one or more of the following, to protect yourself, your family, your house, your car, whatever and whomever you want to protect.

- I invoke the White Light of the Holy Spirit to surround me, my family etc.

- I invoke the blue cloak of Archangel Michael to cover me, my family etc.

- I surround myself with a mirrored sphere, facing outwards to repel all negativity. May only Love and Light, Love and Light, Love and Light enter my force field.

- I place myself in the six pointed star, the Star of David. I invoke the Christ Consciousness to protect me, my family etc.

- I call upon Mother Mary, the feminine energy, to cover me with your blue mantle.

THE MERKABA

Each human body is surrounded not just by an aura. There is an additional field of energy surrounding each human body, called the Merkaba. The Merkaba is a field of energy, a vehicle of light, surrounding the human body for 55 feet, and composed of crystalline and geometric energy. Each and every living thing in the universe is surrounded by a Merkaba, even an atom of a flower.

The earth's Merkaba is like a huge ship or spacecraft, and all the planets have their own Merkaba but also linked into a bigger Merkaba. So each of us is actually enclosed within many Merkabas: our own personal Merkaba; the Merkaba of Planet Earth; the merkaba of the Universe and the Merkaba that surrounds all creation. Known in esoteric knowledge of Ancient Egypt as the 'MER-KA-BA', the name Merkaba is made up of 3 things: MER, meaning Light and referred to in ancient Egypt as love; KA meaning Spirit and BA meaning body.

Merkaba therefore means the Divine Light Vehicle, or the Light Body.

In ancient Egypt the word Merkaba referred to a rotating light that would take the Spirit and the body from one world into another. In Hebrew it means chariot of God. In the bible it is the way Elijah ascended into Heaven.

As a vehicle of light, the Merkaba is capable of transporting our energy upwards to other higher dimensions. It is an ascending vehicle, that can be activated by meditation and breathing.

The Merkaba is composed of 2 tetrahedrons forming a star shape. The pyramid with the point downwards anchors us to the earth, the pyramid with the point upwards raises us up. This star tetrahedron is an amazing and powerful tool, especially during these current times of shifts and transitions. We are presently experiencing enormous changes, like time going faster; people sleeping less or having nightmares or vivid dreams; difficulties in relationships; anxiety attacks. If we activate our electromagnetic field and link into the Merkaba, then we are able to feel better with less diseases. It also gives us the possibility of more psychic powers. It can assist in the connection between the physical and ethereal bodies, allowing us to see the psychological patterns and programs that may limit us, and is a constant reminder to remember our true, loving and Divine nature. By meditating on the Merkaba we are able to merge with Source, the Divine, All That Is.

Mother Earth is constantly trying to re-balance her own magnetic field, which at present is not in balance because of the sun explosions and our abuse of the climate. Human beings will be much more in balance if we activate our own Merkaba.

The Merkaba is alive; it is a living field, not a purely mechanical field of energy. Because it is a living field, it responds to human thought and feeling, which is the way to connect to the field. So the 'computer' that guides the Merkaba is the human mind and heart. The possibilities are endless.

Everything in our reality possesses a star tetrahedral energy field, and planets are no exception. The Star Tetrahedral form of the Merkaba is an immense science that is being studied everywhere throughout the world.

Imagine a child's toy spinning top. As it spins faster, it loses its original shape, becoming a spinning sphere. That's just what your Merkaba looks like.

So consider this. Is it possible that the increasingly frequent sightings of U.F.O.s are actually sightings of Merkabas? After all, the Merkaba is a vehicle, transporting our light energy body to a higher vibration. And there are Merkabas transporting groups of people through all the levels of energy vibration frequencies. Could what we are seeing and thinking to be U.F.O's actually be Merkabas? Could the U.F.O's be the technology of the Merkaba?

Don't just dismiss the idea! Think about it!

Extract from Kryon Book 3, 'Alchemy of the Human Spirit', pages 222-225

(From a live channelling through Lee Carroll)

Some of you have heard about the Merkabah. And you might say, "What is this thing we call the Merkabah?" Now, this is your word; it is not ours. But suffice to say that what we are speaking of is what we call the 'energy shell'. It is that which holds your entire energy together. It is like the skin of your entity, but oh, it's so much more.

You have only seen the Merkabah in history a few times. You are starting to see it more now, and confusing it with ships from space. For it was Elijah who claimed his Merkabah in the field; it glowed, and you saw the wheels within the wheels. You saw the colours, and you saw the magnificence when he ascended. This was the Merkabah that was seen. Each one of you, when you are not here, has a glorious look to you, with colours and vibrations and sounds and shapes all intertwined in the Merkabah, things which you could not possibly see or hear with your biology now for there is so much dimension to the Merkabah, I cannot begin to tell you what it contains.

Now, in the past we have told you that the Merkabah has your colour stripes, those things which tell the other entities of the universe, when they meet you, where you have been and what you have done. And we have told you about the great hall of honour where you received the new colours for being a human on the planet Earth. For it is a wonderful journey that you take. All of you sitting here this night (and reading this) have many stripes from being here so many times. And the great irony is that, although you would come into this room only one time and see these faces of those whom you pretend not to know, at one time they were all your relatives! They are part of your karmic group – brothers, sisters, mothers, fathers: so much has happened between you, and yet you pass as strangers. It is such a wonderful testament to the veil that is here keeping you from seeing the truth, for to truly know these things would cause you to leave.

Oh, dear ones, we honour you for this! Walking the planet in lesson with this veil of not knowing who you are. As we look at you and say to those around us, "They volunteered for this", we love you dearly for it. And so it is that the Merkabah shouts a language that all entities hear, see, feel and experience. So the Merkabah is not just your shell, dear ones; it is your language as well. The Merkabah is the energy which allows you to move from place to place. When you move from one place in the universe to another, it is almost instant, but your Merkabah changes shape to do it. And although we will not get into the science of this, we tell you that it has been channelled before. Look for it, for your Merkabah therefore, is a shape shifter! The shapes that are present in the Merkabah are pure – total – science. And this, dear ones, is a great humorous irony: that your society has chosen to separate the spiritual from the physical, and from the ones who work on your mathematics, and the ones who work on your geometry and your physics.

If you could see the Merkabah, you would understand totally that the relationship is complete and married, for the Merkabah is made of geometry, and it shouts to you your base-12 system. It says that all the shapes are mathematically divisible by six, that there is purpose for this – and yet you still have not seen it. And so we speak of the Merkabah as something grand and glorious. It is owned by you and each one of you has it. But it will not appear on this planet, for to have it would vaporize your biology. The energy is simply too great. And so, short of claiming the Merkabah, you can still work on it, for it still exists in the astral. Part of the steps of being in ascension are to work on it and marry it into your biology.

The Merkabah carries its own light; wherever the Merkabah is, there is light. This makes you creatures of light! Accept it.

Kryon

THE CHAKRA SYSTEM

Our physical body is connected to this physical world, this earthly plane, through our five physical senses. These are the mechanisms through which we are able to experience this world. We see, we hear, we touch, we taste, we smell. We cease to do any of these when we transition back to Spirit, because these are merely physical attributes, appertaining to and belonging to our physical body only.

And how are we connected to all things Spiritual? We are connected to all things Spiritual through our Chakra system. Our chakras exist beyond the physical, but the movement of energy through them is felt in the physical body. The earth too has energy lines, called ley-lines running through it. Our chakras connect us to the universe, to the greater energy field of All That Is. They have been described by Jung as *'the gateways of consciousness'*.

We have seven chakras in all, aligned vertically, from the base of our spine to the crown of our head, running vertically along our spine, spinning and rotating like a Catherine wheel, each drawing in energy from the Great Universal Energy Field, each chakra a different colour, reflecting the seven colours of the rainbow, and each chakra related to a particular aspect of ourselves. This alignment of our seven chakra system along our spine reflects our upward Spiritual development, as we raise our consciousness from our base need for survival, from our base chakra, to our connection to Spirit, through our crown chakra. Each chakra functions as a vortex, continually in motion, drawing cosmic energy into the inner levels of consciousness. When the flow of energy to any chakra is interrupted, that particular chakra becomes blocked, and illness or pain will manifest in the physical body as a result. In esoteric literature, the chakras are often symbolized by the unfolding petals of the lotus flower, which is sacred in India.

Energy meridian lines run from each chakra to the various parts of our body, energising us, in just the same way as blood flows through our veins. It is these meridian lines that are used in acupuncture to re-charge the energy flow around the body.

As well as the seven main chakras, we also have minor chakras or energy centres, for example in the palm of each hand, and in each ear. It is through the palm chakras that the healing energy flows through to the receiver from the holistic practitioner.

Our chakras, just like our aura, send out energy waves that return to us, attracting people of similar minds into our aura. For example, if we suffer from addiction problems, alcohol, gambling, drugs, our sacral chakra, our second chakra from the bottom, sends out the messages and we attract other alcoholics and drug users into our lives. On the other hand, if we are highly Spiritually aware, our crown chakra, our connection to the divine, to Spirit, emits the signals, and we magnetise people to us who are on a similar Spiritual path to our own.

In order to operate fully, our chakras need to be balanced, which means they all need to be spinning at the same speed. They need to be constantly cleansed, re-balanced and re-energised. Here is a meditation exercise to help you.

ENERGISING YOUR CHAKRAS

- Sit quietly. Close your eyes. Relax your body. Concentrate on your breathing.

- Starting with your base chakra, imagine it as a tiny bud, opening out into a red flower. Draw the White Light down into it, watching it rotate in an anti-clockwise direction.

- Now move to your sacral chakra, see an orange flower opening up and rotating as you draw the White Light into it.

- Now move to your solar plexus, imagine a yellow flower opening up and rotating as the White Light is drawn into it.

- Now move to your heart chakras, pink and green, and feel the White Light expanding and rotating them.

- Now move to your throat chakra, blue. Feel it open out and rotate as the White Light enters it.

- Now move to your Third Eye Chakra, an indigo flower opening out and rotating.

- Finally, move to your crown chakra, violet, flowering out and rotating.

- Now imagine all your chakras rotating all at the same speed.

- When you are ready, begin to close your chakras down again.

- Starting with your base chakra, withdraw each flower back into its bud state again and seal each bud..

- Work upwards to your crown chakra.

- When you are ready, open your eyes.

**CLEANSING, RESTORING AND BALANCING YOUR CHAKRAS
WITH THE ARCHANGELS**

- Sit quietly. Close your eyes. Relax your body. Concentrate on your breathing.

- Ground and protect yourself.

- Call upon Archangel Sandalphon to cleanse and restore your base chakra. See your red base chakra rotating, being cleansed and restored. Thank Archangel Sandalphon.

- Call upon Archangel Chamuel to cleanse and restore your sacral chakra. See your orange sacral chakra rotating, being cleansed and restored. Ask Archangel Chamuel to balance it with your base red chakra. Thank Archangel Chamuel.

- Call upon Archangel Uriel to cleanse and restore your solar plexus. See your yellow third chakra rotating, being cleansed and restored. Ask Archangel Uriel to balance this chakra with the other two, so that all three are rotating ta the same speed. Thank Archangel Uriel.

- Call upon Archangel Chamuel and Raphael to cleanse and restore your heart chakra, which has two colours, pink and green. Ask Chamuel to work on the pink for love at a cosmic level, and Raphael on the green for love at a personal level. Ask that the heart chakra be balanced with the other three, so that all four are rotating at the same speed.

- Call upon Archangel Michael to cleanse and restore your throat chakra, your blue chakra. Sense it being cleansed and restored, and ask Michael to balance it with the other four chakras.

- Call upon Archangel Gabriel again to cleanse and restore your third eye chakra, your indigo chakra. Ask that this too be balanced with the other five chakras.

- Call upon Archangel Zadkiel to cleanse and restore your crown chakra, your violet chakra, your connection to Spirit. Sense your crown chakra being cleansed and restored. Ask Zadkiel to balance this chakra with all the other six chakras.

See all your chakras now rotating at the same speed, red, orange, yellow, green/pink, blue, indigo violet.

Feel the energy circulating through you as all your chakras rotate at the same speed.

- When you are ready, ask the Archangels to close each chakra and seal it.

- Thank your Archangels and open your eyes.

KUNDALINI

Kundalini is the force of the divine, intelligent life-force (Prana) that resides in all of us. Like a serpent, Kundalini awakens from its sleep at the base of the spine and slowly rises. Once awakened, Kundalini energy opens and strengthens the root chakra and spirals upwards. In its snake-like form, it circles and clears all the chakras, releasing blocks and allowing the energy to flow smoothly. It is a very hot, powerful energy and can assist with Spiritual awakening and divine communication.

In Sanskrit, Kundalini translates to "coiled up, coils, the coiled power" and is often represented in drawings as a snake or serpent that rests coiled around the base of the spine, at the root chakra.

This energy remains dormant unless awakened (known as Kundalini Awakening). Kundalini Awakening can happen through the attunement process or simply through meditation and/or prayer. Sometimes it comes suddenly and spontaneously, such as by a near-death experience.

When we waken the Kundalini energy, and it can certainly be done in this life-time, the serpent will uncoil upwards in a spiral movement, awakening the chakras up to and including the crown chakra, in an explosive enlightening.

Occasionally the person will be aware as the subconscious unveils and there is a vast increase in knowledge and awareness. Normally this is not instant or immediate, although it can be.

So, as we can see, there is a lot more to us than we realise! We are a lot more than what we think we are!

We are not just our physical body. In fact, as we have seen, we *are* not a physical body at all. We *have* a physical body, at the same time as we *are* an energy body, which is composed of an emotional body, a mental body, and a Spiritual body sometimes called an astral body, all of which contain all our past experiences, even past lives. We have subtle bodies of higher frequencies which correspond to pure divine expressions of universal will, love and wisdom.

However, even though we are Spiritual beings, we are at this present time experiencing a physical existence on Planet Earth. We need to stay grounded in this dimension, otherwise we would be up in the clouds all the time, unable to cope with life. We need to ground our energy! Come down to earth! We need to stabilize ourselves in Mother Earth!

So how do we put all of this into the context of living a life of joy and inner peace, regardless of what life throws at us?

Well, if we have *self-knowledge,* if we know and accept that we are each a Spiritual being, and not just a physical body, and if we accept that our Spiritual body is our real essence and immortal, while our physical body will eventually decay, then we will surely see the sense in paying more attention to that immortal part of us!

As Yeshua tells us in the Gospel of Thomas, Logion 56:

"Yeshua said: / 'Whoever knows the world / discovers a corpse. / And whoever discovers a corpse / cannot be contained by the world.'"

Meaning that if we attempt to live in the world without acknowledging and accepting our Spiritual dimension, that dimension that makes us complete and whole, we are lifeless, just like a corpse. A corpse after all, is just a physical body from where the soul, the life force, has exited. Our body without our soul cannot exist. It is the soul that gives life to us.

And:

"Yeshua said: / 'When you see someone who was not born from a womb, then prostrate yourselves and give worship, for this is your Father'."

In other words, while our physical body is born from a womb, and therefore subject to decay and decomposition in what we call death, our soul on the other hand is eternal, that immortal, everlasting, unlimited part of us that is our divine essence, our God energy.

Furthermore, when we realise all that we actually are, the forces within us, and the subtle energies surrounding us, interconnecting constantly with us, then we can live life to its full potential. When we understand everything that we truly are, when we understand the whole of what we truly are, then it is not rocket science to see how we can live life to the full, as we are meant to do, rather than struggling in a limited playing field where all the odds appear to be stacked against us.

And if we could just see ourselves and each other as the bright Spiritual light each of us really is, a conductor of Divine Light, then we would not judge, we would not criticise, we would not condemn. And just think of all the weight lifted from us if we could release ourselves from the burden of all of that!

What a wonder man is! As Shakespeare's Hamlet said:

'What a piece of work is man! How noble in reason! How infinite in faculty! In form and movement how express and admirable! In action how like an angel! In apprehension how like a god! The beauty of the world! The paragon of animals!'

And yet, at the same time:

'....... this godly frame, the earth, seems to me a sterile promontory, this most excellent canopy, the air, look you, this brave o'erhanging firmament, this majestical roof fretted with golden fire - why, it appears no other thing to me than a foul and pestilent congregation of vapours.'

In other words, there is much more to us than we realise, and much more that we need to understand about the nature of this world and our reason for being here.

In the Gospel of Thomas we read:

"Yeshua said: / 'If they ask you from whence you come, say: / We were born of the Light, / there where Light is born of Light, / It holds true and is revealed within their image. / If they ask you who you are, say: / We are its children, / the beloved of the Father, the Loving One. / If they ask you what is the sign of the Father in you, say: / It is movement and it is repose'. " (Logion 50)

So, who am I? Where do I come from? Where am I going? Questions that concern us all! Jesus himself answers them for us!

We are the Light. We have come from the Light. And we are going towards the Light. And as we are awaken as a whole to the divinity which each one of us is, as we become aware of and acknowledge our own God Essence as we are awakening to the vast unlimited aspects of ourselves.

Jesus told us, *'Know yourself and you will know everything!'*

You are the source of everything. You are where everything is stored. There is a living library, an infinite source of knowledge within you.

In other words, within you is ALL.

CHAPTER 2:

At-One-Ment

We have just seen that everything, absolutely everything is energy, including ourselves as human beings, and the only difference between us all is the speed at which our energy moves and the vibrational energy frequency on which each of us operates. We, as humans, are just energy moving at a slower speed. As energy slows down, it gathers molecules which becomes matter, or mass. Hence we materialise as mass or matter in this earth dimension or earth plane, where the energy is slowed right down to the most dense.

Science has also shown us that energy manifests at the same time as a wave (energy) and a particle (matter or mass). So we, as energy, are both wave and matter or mass. The mass part of us is our physical body and the energy or wave part of us is our energy body, our soul or Spirit.

And we have just seen too how our physical body is contained or is nesting within our energy body, those four energy layers that surround our physical body. This energy body we all *are* is as individual and as unique as is our physical body, our energy body being an integral and inseparable part of us.

And it is this energy body that connects each one of us to the Great Universal Energy Field, the Great Universal Consciousness, the Great Universal Force, the Great Universal God Energy, the Light, the Universal Mind, the Universal Intelligence, call it whatever, outside of which nothing and no one can possibly exist. The

Universal God Energy, omniscient, omnipresent, and omnipotent, overseeing and overshadowing absolutely everything in the entirety and infinity of creation. This Universal Mind, this Universal Intelligence, is everywhere and is not separate from anything. This Universal Mind, this Universal Intelligence is the life force of every atom, every molecule, every electron that is in existence. The source of pure potential in a limitless playing field.

This Great Universal God Energy, this Great Universal Consciousness, call it what you will, connects all of creation. Holographic in nature, it is a universal container, in which every part is connected to every other part, each part mirroring and reflecting the whole on a smaller scale.

Just like everything else, the human energy body emerges out of this Great Universal God Energy Field, and having emerged from it, remains connected to it. This is the life-line, just like the babe in the womb connected to the mother for sustenance and life itself. This Universal God Energy is infinitely and endlessly creative, manifesting in countless upon countless forms of life, forms of slowed-down energy, in all its splendour, magnificence, self-sufficiency, abundance, beauty, intelligence and love.

And how do we continue to communicate with this Great Universal Consciousness, of which we are a part and not apart from? We communicate not through language, language being a device of this dense earth vibration only. We communicate with this Great Universal God Energy through our thoughts. Unconditional loving thoughts, thoughts with absolutely no conditions attached, loving attitudes and loving beliefs all result in more enhancing and harmonious life experiences. Conversely, non-harmony, discord, lack and limitation all stem from fear. And what is fear? Fear is the opposite of love. This Great Universal Consciousness is Love. God is Love. Fear is separation from this Great Universal Life Force, lack of trust in this all-encompassing Universal Consciousness. Every thought we have goes out into this Great Universal Field of Energy, and brings back similar to us from this same Great Universal Energy Field. It is a two-way system. We feed from it and we contribute to it. And to tap into this Great Universal Energy Field, we must see ourselves as an inherent part of it and not apart from it.

And this is what we need to come to terms with, this is what we need to get into our heads, if we are going to be able to make any progress along our Spiritual path. One of the main discoveries of quantum physics is, put simply, that the universe does not exist somewhere *"out there,"* separate from us. Quantum physics has proven, again and again, that there is no objective, independent universe which we can passively and objectively observe. We are all One in the vastness of the entirety of creation, we are all of the same Great Universal Energy Field. And being from the same Great Universal Energy Field, and remaining connected to it, that means we are all connected to each other within this Great Universal God Energy. Yes, everything not just in our world, but in the entirety of creation is indeed connected to everything else, and inseparably connected

The human body is only the visible, earthly part of a greater whole, as we have seen in the first chapter, a greater whole, a greater Life Force that surrounds it, interpenetrates it and gives it life. This Great Universal Field of Energy permeates all that surrounds us, both visibly and invisibly, the human energy body being one of the manifestations of this Great Universal Energy we call God. So each one of us is therefore, a manifestation, an outlet for this Universal Consciousness, this Infinite Energy. Each one of us is an expression of God.

The word **atonement** is often misunderstood. Many take it to mean compensating for or making up for some misdeed. But the real meaning of the word?

At-One-Ment.

Now when we look at it like this, we get a very different understanding. In this world, there is only fear and love. As we have just seen, fear is simply the separation from the Great Universal God Energy, love is living in the wholeness of the Great Universal God Energy. So we have a choice! Do we choose to live in fear or do we choose to live in love?

At-One-Ment means letting go of the world of fear and returning to the world of love, leaving the world of separation and returning to the world of wholeness. It means living in the vastness and greatness of the wholeness, in the magnificence of our true identity rather than struggling in the limited identity of the small body or ego. It is the getting rid of the illusions of death, sin and loss and coming into our own natural state of harmony and peace, in the **Oneness** that is **All.**

Consider all the electrical gadgets and machines you have in your home. They all run on electricity, their source of power, without which they cannot possibly operate or function.

Each machine or gadget performs a different task for you, each has an individual role to play in keeping your home functioning. Even though each is diverse and individual, they are all, each and every one, connected to and plugged into the one source of power, the main great electricity grid.

So too, we, as individual forms of energy, are all connected to the main great universal source of energy. We are all wired up with the connecting wires, and fully connected to the great operating system, the great source of energy. And this main source of energy is the Great Universal Consciousness, the Great Universal God Energy. Yes, as we have seen, God is an energy, but not just any energy! *THEE* energy! *THEE* energy that incorporates all other forms of energy in the entirety of creation, anything or anyone that is, that ever has been, and that ever will be.

The great seventeenth century Romantic poet, William Wordsworth explains:

'A presence that is not to be put by........a motion and a spirit that impels / All living things, all objects of all thoughts / And rolls through all things.'

And Einstein too put forward the idea that there is a common, universal energy consciousness that animates all things, and therefore interconnects all things.

In order to function properly, we need to be plugged into this universal system. In fact, we cannot operate or exist outside of this Great Universal Energy that we call God. We only exist because this God energy exists. And the way in which we operate within this Great Universal Energy is through our thoughts and our feelings.

Look at it this way. The wave is in the ocean. The wave is only there because the ocean is there. The ocean has given life to the wave, and the wave has no possibility of existing outside of the ocean. The wave *IS* the ocean, but it is not the ocean in the ocean's entirety. The ocean throws up the wave, which grows and develops, then crashes and is no longer a wave. But it is still in the ocean. It has not gone anywhere. It has just changed energy form. Each and every wave is individual, no two are exactly alike. The ocean does not dictate to the wave how to develop. And there is no such thing as a perfect wave! And there are no two waves the same! Each is unique in itself.

So it is with us and the Great God Energy. We are all contained within the Oneness of that Great God Energy, that Great Universal God Consciousness. And within that Oneness, we each have an individual identity, an individual energy, operating on a particular vibrational energy frequency level, depending on our Spiritual awareness, our own Soul consciousness, and how far up the ladder we are in the whole understanding of the concept of God, our understanding of the whole concept of energy, the meaning of life and why we are here on this dense earth energy dimension.

Consider this too. Imagine you dip your finger in the ocean and take out a tiny little drop of water on the tip of your finger. That tiny little droplet of water contains all the elements of the entire ocean. It has the salty taste, the essence, everything the ocean has. But it is not the entire ocean in the ocean's entirety.

Or consider the fog. The fog throws up all sorts of shapes that continually change form, merge and separate, but always remaining within the fog. Outside of the fog, they have no existence. They must remain within that Oneness of the fog, but within that Oneness they are free to take any form they wish, constantly changing and reforming.

And within the Great Universal God Energy, that Great Universal **Oneness**, just like the wave in the ocean, or the shapes in the fog, we have the freedom to act as we wish. Mankind has been endowed with the gift and privilege of free will. But with every gift and privilege there comes the responsibility to use that for the highest good of all. And here is where the problems in this world begin. Man's free will has run rampant! Simply because man has lost the connection with the Great Universal God Energy. Yes, we are still in that great Universal God Energy, simply because, as we have seen, there is no place else for us to exist. But we have lost our understanding of what it all means!

So we can see that God is **THEE** universal energy, incorporating all forms of life that are, that ever have been and that ever will be. The **Oneness** of **All That Is.**

At-One-Ment is simply another word for Collective Consciousness or Unity Consciousness. And that Collective Consciousness or Unity Consciousness is what we call God.

And within that Collective Consciousness, that Oneness we call God, there is no such thing as chance or coincidence. There is only synchronicity. Synchronicity is the result of Unity Consciousness, where everything flows freely and in order to a Divine plan. Within the Oneness there is no *'I'* or *'me'* or 'mine'. There is only *'we'.*

Now let us consider this. Just as the small droplet of water from the ocean, or the wave in the same ocean *are* the ocean, but not the ocean in the entirety of the ocean, and just as the shapes in the fog *are* the fog, but each one is not the entire fog, all the combined shapes forming the fog, then each one of us, being in the Great Universal God Energy, *is* God, in the sense that we contain all the elements of the God Essence. Each one of us is not God in God's entirety, but combined, we make up the entirety of God.

And when we live in the **Oneness**, we are powerful and magnificent beings.

But, before you ask, - yes, we must be in the **Oneness**, because there is nowhere else for us to exist! But there is existing and there is thriving! Two very different things!

Back to the electricity in your home again! Your home is wired up for the electricity, just as the television channels are in your home. But you need to be connected by having the switch turned on or the channel tuned in! Right?

So too, even though you are already wired up for the system, you need to be connected to the Great Universal God Energy, switched on, tuned in, whatever.

And how do you know if you are connected? There is one question you need to ask, and that one question is, am I happy in what I am doing? Am I doing what I love doing and do I love doing what I am doing?

If the answer to this question, in any department of your life, is hesitant, or a no, then you are not as fully connected as you should be.

And the result is you are not happy! So to be happy, you have to get connected! And to get connected you have to first separate yourself from the person or situation that is not bringing you happiness and get into a situation where you will be happy, where you will be at peace with yourself, where you will be in the **Oneness.**

When we live in the **Oneness**, we are limitless beings. And when we realise this, why would we remain in the limited world of the individual when we can live in the limitless expanse of the entirety of the **Oneness**? It's not rocket science to work this out!

And living in the **Oneness** means we are all **One**! I am you and you are me. What I do to someone else, I do to myself. There is no separation. **Oneness** means just that, **Oneness.** Or in another word, **At-one-ment**.

We are all connected, all inter-linked, all inter-dependent, all inter-mingling as the One Great Energy. We need one another in order to survive. And we need all other forms of life in order to survive. What affects one, affects all.

Take the trees for example. They give us the oxygen we need to breathe, and we give them the carbon dioxide which in turn they need to breathe. We are in the trees, the trees are in us. We operate together, in a cyclical movement, the cycle of life. The trees are our inbreath, and our outbreath gives the trees their inbreath. As we breathe out, they breathe in. Natural re-cycled air conditioning! We give and take from each other in the great cycle of life and living. Every single species, every single form of life, every stone, whatever its level of consciousness, contributes to and has a purpose in the Great Universal Energy, in the great plan of all Creation, in the Great Universal Intelligence.

Consider the sheet of paper you hold in your hand. Where has it come from? Look at all the cosmic forces at work, all the cosmic forces that have come together to bring that sheet of paper into manifestation. The trees, whose inbreath, as we have just seen, is our outbreath; the soil and the earth that support the trees; the clouds overhead that transmute into rain to nurture the growth of the trees; the sun that nourishes the trees and enables them to grow.

Life is an endless flow of energy, that same flow of energy connecting everyone, everywhere, simultaneously, uniting us all as One Consciousness. And within that One Consciousness, everything responds and reacts to everything else. The true inter-connectedness, the true inter-being of every living thing cannot be over-estimated.

In the Gospel of Mary of Magdala, one of the Nag Hammadi scripts, we read:

"The Saviour replied: 'Every nature, every modeled form, every creature, exists in and with each other.' "

And William Blake, poet and mystic, 1757-1827 writes:

'To see a World in a Grain of Sand, / And a Heaven in a Wild Flower, / Hold Infinity in the palm of your hand, / And Eternity in an hour.'

Yes, every thing is contained in every other thing!

And in *Auguries of Innocence'* Blake warns us of the disastrous consequences for man if we hurt or harm any living thing. Any sort of cruelty to even the most tiny of beings, such as an ant, will shake the fabric of the whole universe, being contrary to the natural law which respects all life equally.

And in '*On Another's Sorrow*':

'Can I see another's woe, / And not be in sorrow too? / Can I see another's grief, / And not seek for kind relief?'

Yes, we are all connected!

The poet Gerard Manley Hopkins, born in 1844 in London, in his poem '*Binsey Poplars*' tells us:

'O if we but knew what we do / When we delve or hew - / Hack and rack the growing green! / Since country is so tender / To touch her being so slender, / That, like this sleek and seeing ball / But a prick will make no eye at all, / Where we, even when we mean / To mend her we end her / When we hew or delve.'

Hopkins' complex doctrine was that of '*instress'* and '*inscape'*, derived partly from medieval philosophers, in which the distinctive design or patterning of anything echoes its reason for existence and its uniqueness. Everything has a pattern, a blue-print pattern. And that blue-print works in a cyclical form. For example, an identical leaf appears each year on each particular branch in the same place as the previous year. In other words, the physical etheric leaf, as with all forms of life, holds its pattern in cyclical motion. That's why our children look like us! The etheric life-form holds its pattern.

And it is indeed true that if a butterfly flaps its wings in South America, that has a knock-on effect on all of us. Our souls are all One Soul, just dressed in different guises.

We are not separate from the earth. We **are** the earth. Everything we do to the earth, we do to ourselves. There is only *one* Universal Consciousness, and as we destroy any part of that whatsoever, the other parts are affected. And when we awaken to the fact that we and the universe are One, then and only then will we realise our greatness within the unlimited Oneness and realise our unlimited potentiality. This is what humanity is here to learn, to live in harmony with all life, all people, all nature. And when we eventually learn this lesson, the earth's unlimited sources of abundance will flow freely to all. Hiding in what we consider to be our reality of separateness is grossly hindering our Spiritual advancement, keeping us in an on-going state of belief in want and scarcity, which is where we find ourselves when we continue to ignore the forces of nature who are here to support us and work with us, but whom we insist on destroying and exploiting regardless of the consequences. In destroying nature and its forces, we seem to have not yet worked out that we are destroying ourselves, destroying the very source of our life-giving sustenance!

And in this connectedness of the One Great Universal Consciousness, the health of one is connected to the health of all. If we destroy our natural environment with all its life-giving and life-sustaining substances, how can we expect to remain healthy? Our bodies mirror, reflect and respond to our environment.

Everything living has a consciousness and an inherent life-force. When we destroy any of that life-force, then the result is that we are drinking 'dead' water and eating 'dead' food. When we destroy the rain forests and the trees around us, we are starving ourselves of oxygen. And then we wonder why there is so much illness and dis-ease on this Planet Earth! Why there are so many forms of respiratory problems affecting so many people!

And, as we have seen, it is not just on this earth plane or universe that we are all connected. All of creation, the entire cosmos throughout time and space, absolutely all of it! All is connected in the great web of life, the Metatron Cube, which holds all together in the greatest, the most elaborate, the most intricate network of sound, mathematical equations and geometrical designs. Most people are now realizing and accepting the truth that the solar system has a profound relationship to our physical body and our other lighter bodies. We are a microcosm of the macrocosm of all creation, and as such, just a smaller version, but similar in every way. That is what is meant by the phrase, *'As within, so without; as above, so below'*. Anything that goes on in our solar system has an effect on our own chakra system and on all our lighter bodies, not just our physical body.

For example, we all know that the moon affects our moods, it pulls the tides in and out, the sun gives life to our crops, the clouds supply the rain to grow those crops. Is the inter-connectedness of all things not blatantly obvious? And feeling *'Under the weather'* is something with which we can certainly all identify! Consider all the pains and aches most people have and how they all suffer more in the damp weather! Even the curls in my hair have always turned fuzzy before the rain comes! I am my own weather barometer! Cool or what!

Yes, we see and feel it every day! What goes on out there in the ether affects us all here! And it has been very noticeable lately. More and more people are now experiencing various symptoms, such as lack of sleep, dehydration, lucid dreams or nightmares, ears ringing, dizziness, aches and pains, headaches, low energy, apathy, inexplicable irritability and anxiety, palpitations or sweatings. These are all coming from forces and energy fields outside of ourselves, but inter-relating with us, as with all creation. When we realise and understand all of this, then we understand that it will all pass, just like a storm or hurricane. Everything passes. We just need to hold the Light, and that simply means remaining positive, instead of adding to the turmoil by sending out any more negative vibrations of anxiety, fear and panic. It is all under control! Everything is as it should be! Trust in the Great Universal Mind!

Indeed, we are all in the **Oneness**, the **Oneness** of the Great Universal God Energy, the Great Universal God Consciousness, all inter-linked, the only difference being the particular energy vibrational frequency on which each of us operates. Each of us is a unique expression of the Great Universal Energy we call God. The same energy that flows through my veins in the form of blood is akin to the energy that flows through the branches of the trees in the form of sap, and akin to the energy that blows through those same branches in the form of wind. I am just another particular and unique expression of the energy of **All That Is**. And there are no two of us who give expression to that creative energy in the same way.

And so, if I am you and you are me, then why would I want to hurt you? I am only hurting myself! Why would I be jealous of you? How can I be jealous of myself? And I certainly would not want to kill you! In the words of the battle cry of the infamous three musketeers: 'All for *One* and *One* for all!'

But, ironically, we end up killing each other! We think of ourselves as technologically advanced. But our technology is being used to produce weapons of destruction which we aim at each other! Technology was meant to help us and advance our lives, but we have reversed all that, grossly mis-using earth's natural resources for our own devious ends. We are destroying the very lives we should be improving and the very earth of which we should be the custodians!

And all because we see ourselves as separate entities, fighting each other through fear that if you get more, then I must be getting less, or I am going to kill you before you kill me.

The Gospel of Thomas, another of the texts found at Nag Hammadi, tells us:

"His disciples said to him: / 'When will the new world come?' / He answered them: / 'What you are waiting for has already come, but you do not see it'." (Logion 51, Gospel of Thomas)

What we are searching for, that peace, harmony and fulfilment for which we yearn, is already within us. It is not something that will come some day; it is already here and now. It is always here and now. To search for it elsewhere is to be separate from it. But it is a dimension of our present life, a part of and not apart from, ourselves.

In the universal and cosmic **Oneness,** everything you can imagine and experience is within you. All that you seek, you already are! And if we operate from this point, then we are guaranteed a happy, harmonious life!

In the Gospel of Thomas we read:

'If you do not fast from the world, you will not find the Kingdom.'

And the bible tells us:

'In God we live and move and have our being.' (Acts: 17-28)

And how can God be defined? God is NOT a person, God is NOT any sort of being.

God can be defined in just two words. And those two words?

GOD IS.

And how do you define yourself? You can only define yourself within that **Beingness,** that state of **Being,** or that state of consciousness we call God, again with just two words. *I AM.* That is the only way that you can ever define yourself!

'Sure I'm only human!' An opt-out phrase if ever there was one! We are not only human, and by claiming to be only human, we are limiting ourselves and denying our divine greatness in the Oneness of All That Is.

In the Gospel of Thomas we read:

"Yeshua told him (Thomas): / 'I am no longer your Master, because you have drunk, and become drunken / from the same bubbling source from which I spring'."

Yeshua has recognised and acknowledged Thomas as one who has attained self-knowledge through the realisation that we all come from the same Source and we are all **One within that Source.**

And from the same Gospel:

"Yeshua said: /'This sky will pass away, / and the one above it will also pass away. / The dead have no life, / and the living have no death. / On days when you ate what was dead, you made it alive. / When you are in the light, what will you do?/ When you were One, you created two. / But now that you are two, what will you do?' "
(Logion 11)

Here Yeshua is reminding us that everything will pass. Everything that has a beginning must have an end. Our physicality will pass. And then we return to Unity, having completed our passage of learning through the duality process that we brought upon ourselves, as a necessary soul process of maturing and evolving, bringing us back to Unity with the One. We cannot continue to exist in duality, that too is only a temporary, passing phase.

A young child does not live in duality, not yet separated completely from Source. Yeshua tells us, again in the Gospel of Thomas, Logion 4:

'An aged person will not hesitate to ask a seven-day-old infant about the Place of Life, and that person will live. / Many of the first will make themselves last, and they will become One.'

Yeshua here is reminding us about the Divine Child, the innocent, pure, uncontaminated part of us that is always in the Oneness, and by acknowledging this Child within us, we see the world through the joyous eyes of a child, through the joyous eyes of Source, through the joyous and unlimited scope of living in the **Oneness** of **All That Is.**

The theoretical quantum physicist, Dr. Amit Goswami, a prolific writer, teacher and visionary, is one of a number of scientists who in recent years, has ventured into the domain of the Spiritual in an attempt to validate intuitions about the existence of a Spiritual dimension of life. Goswami writes:

'When we understand us, our consciousness, we also understand the universe and the separation disappears.'

At-One-Ment, in the Oneness of the Great Universal God Energy, the Great Universal Consciousness, with everything in the entirety of all creation, is the only place we can ever be! There is nowhere else!

I *am that I am!*

'I AM' AFFIRMATIONS

- I AM THAT I AM THAT I AM
- I AM LIGHT
- I AM TRUTH
- I AM DIVINE ESSENCE
- I AM THE DIVINE MADE MANIFEST
- I AM PERFECT HEALTH
- I AM ABUNDANCE
- I AM ETERNAL LOVE
- I AM DIVINE CREATION
- I AM DIVINE WISDOM
- I AM THE BREATH OF LIFE
- I AM UNCONDITIONAL LOVE
- I AM ONE WITH THE SOURCE
- I AM DIVINE LIGHT IN HUMAN FORM
- I AM DIVINE WILL
- I AM IN MY VIOLET FLAME
- I AM STRONG
- I AM GRATITUDE
- I AM PEACE
- I AM PERFECT DESIGN
- I AM ONE WITH THE SOURCE OF ALL LIFE
- I AM

NAMASTE

I honour the place in You

Where the entire Universe dwells.

I honour the place in You

Which is of Love

Of Truth

Of Light

And

Of Peace.

When you are in that place in You

And I AM in that place in Me

We are One.

MEDITATION FOR CONNECTING WITH DIVINE ENERGY

- Sit quietly. Relax your body. Concentrate on your breathing. Clear your mind.

- Slow down your breathing, in, out, in, out, slowly, relaxed, rhythmically.

- As you breathe in, visualise yourself breathing in the White Light of God, harmonising your whole being, as you take in the Divine energy, absorbing the stream of God Light.

- As you breathe out, project the breath of God out to the earth, blessing all others and all life forms.

- Keep breathing until you can feel that you are breathing in rhythm with the universal life stream of energy, that you are not just breathing in and out, but that you, too, are being breathed in and out by a much greater life force, in rhythm with all other life forms on the Planet and in the universe. There is one breath, one life. You are now strongly connected to the Universal Life Energy, the Divine Energy.

- Continue to breathe, slowly, harmoniously; as you inhale, feel the God-breath filling you, and as you exhale, bless all life.

- Expand your consciousness outside your own body, to the space all around you, as far out on all sides as you can. Continue your breathing.

- When you are ready, give thanks to Spirit and open your eyes.

CONNECTING YOURSELF TO THE UNIVERSAL ENERGY
WITH ARCHANGEL SANDALPHON

- Sit quietly. Close your eyes. Relax your body. Concentrate on your breathing.

- Call in Archangel Sandalphon to help you connect to Mother Earth.

- Imagine Sandalphon's amber sphere travelling from your base chakra, down through your legs and feet, right down into Mother Earth. Feel your connection with Mother Earth.

- Breathe in deeply, absorbing the earth's energy, right up through your whole body, and as you breathe out, expel all the negativity from your body back down into Mother Earth again.

- Repeat three times.

- Now draw the amber ball back up through your feet, your legs, right up through your whole body, up through your crown chakra, up into the celestial realms. Feel the connection.

- Breathe in deeply, absorbing this celestial energy, drawing it right down through your whole body, down into the earth.

- Repeat three times.

- Now, simultaneously, draw in the energy from the earth up through your feet, and the energy from the heavenly kingdom down through your body, merging the two and circulating them all through your body

- You are now connected both to the Earth energy and the Celestial energy. Feel the flow of this universal energy down and through your body.

- When you are ready, thank Mother Earth and thank the Heavenly Realms.

- Open your eyes, feeling your body full of light energy, the Universal Energy.

CONNECTING WITH MOTHER EARTH

- Sit quietly. Close your eyes. Relax your body. Concentrate on your breathing.

- Imagine yourself travelling down through the soles of your feet, down and down through all the earth's layers, as far as you can go towards the centre of the earth, until you come to a bright clearing.

- Look around you at the beauty of the trees, the crystals, the rocks, the water, breathing in all the goodness, all the light.

- Listen to the caressing, motherly voice of Lady Gaia, Mother Earth, as she welcomes you. Soak in the beauty around you.

- Spend your time with Mother Earth. You don't need to speak. Mother Earth can read your thoughts. Just open your heart to her. Ask her how you can serve.

- When you are ready, thank Mother Earth for this connection and begin your journey back up through your body again.

- Open your eyes. Feel stronger for having made the connection.

CHAPTER 3:

A soul's sole mission - why we are here

We are first and foremost Spiritual beings, Spiritual beings having a physical experience for the duration of this life-time. We are here on a mission. And that mission is not a mission to acquire as much material wealth and possessions as we possibly can in the short space of earthly time allotted to us. Our sole reason for being here on this earth dimension, on this earth energy vibration is to evolve our immortal soul, to raise our own Spiritual consciousness and the collective Spiritual consciousness of all humanity. Consciousness is a state of being, which is actually more solid than the dense physical places that we see here all around us on this earth. We are here to move ourselves up in vibration, towards ascension. But we cannot ascend alone, we must ascend collectively. So as we move into the higher dimensions, those higher frequency vibrations will bring us all into Unity Consciousness. Unity Consciousness carries us all, so that all life advances, as we all accelerate and ascend collectively, as One.

Earth is a learning school for us all. We have freely chosen to be here, yet again, in order to learn the lessons which we have freely chosen to learn this time around. If we do not learn the lesson as it is presented to us, it will re-appear time after time in a different form and through a different person or situation until we do learn it. For example, we often find ourselves attracting the same type of partner time and time again. The one who criticises us, puts us down, deflates our self-confidence, perhaps even physically or mentally abuses us. The lesson here is one of self-respect. Until you decide that no-one is ever going to do this to you again, that you are worth only the best, that you value yourself, then you will continue to attract a partner who will repeat and continue that same behaviour towards you, until you learn that particular lesson of self-respect, self-love and self-worth.

During our in-between-life-time periods, when we are in a higher Spiritual dimension, we decide whether or not we wish to return to this earth dimension. We have a choice. It is always our free choice. No one forces us to do anything. And why would we wish to return? Why would we wish to leave the higher Spiritual vibrations of unconditional love, joy and peace to return to this earth dimension? Simply because this earth dimension is the most dense of all the energy vibration frequencies, and so it is here the most lessons are to be learned, lessons which will evolve our immortal soul. For example, it is only on this dense earth vibration frequency that war, hatred, envy, greed, lust for power and control and all the other negative attributes exist. We can of course remain in the higher vibration Spiritual frequencies and progress there. But if we want to fast-track our soul evolutionary progress, then another round on this dense earth dimension will certainly help! And it will help even more, we will collect even more brownie points if we choose a difficult journey!

For example, why would anyone choose to live a life of homelessness and poverty on the streets of London or any other large city, when they could have chosen a life of luxury and comfort?

Well, that decision, as are all decisions, was made at soul level between that person and other members of his soul family. We are here to spread love and to help each other as best we can. Each one of us is either the person who instigates the action or the person on whom the action is perpetrated. Each one of us is simultaneously both cause and effect.

That homeless man on the streets has certainly chosen a very difficult path. And in choosing that difficult path, he is probably a very Spiritually advanced being, sacrificing his own comfort this time around by offering us the opportunity to give and to help. Our souls cry out to help and to be of service, and in order to be able to help, then there needs to be people in need of help. Right? For example, we cannot help earthquake victims until an earthquake happens. We cannot help famine victims until a famine occurs. All these what we call disasters provide us with a wake-up call! They give each of us the opportunity to evolve our Spiritual consciousness by responding with love, compassion and caring. The very reason why we are here in the first place! And when we fail to respond, we have just missed a golden opportunity to raise our Spiritual awareness! Not to mention how we have just negated and poured cold water on the sacrifice made by those who volunteered to help us by offering us that opportunity!

And as we will see later, the universe is a mirror, mirroring or reflecting what is inside each of us. So all that violence, all that aggression, all those earthquakes and other natural disasters tell us a lot about the state of our feelings and thoughts, those negative thoughts and feelings which keep us trapped in the base consciousness level.

Nothing whatsoever is left to chance when we are planning our life blue-print. Every detail is taken care of, even down to selecting our parents. Especially when selecting our parents! If we have chosen to learn certain lessons, then it makes perfect sense that we choose a set of parents who are going to be instrumental in teaching us those lessons. For example, if I decide that I would like to evolve my immortal soul by being abused in some way as a child, possibly in order to bring that particular offence to public world-wide attention in order to save others from suffering in the same way, then I have got to make certain that I select parents who have agreed to play out that role.

Yes, we are all game-players in the drama of life! We all play the role we have agreed to play this time around in order, not just to evolve our own immortal soul, but also to help others evolve Spiritually as well. That is why we can never judge anyone, simply because we do not know what role anyone has agreed to play this time around. I am not for one second condoning any sort of abusive behaviour, violence or murder on the part of anyone. What I am saying is that there is always, not an excuse, but an explanation, for that behaviour, an excuse and an explanation being two very different things. We are not privy to enough information about anyone else's life plan to enable us to judge anyone for their actions.

So, when we understand fully why we are here on this earth plane at this particular time, it is much easier for us to go with the flow and not get upset about the little insignificant things that occur in our lives but which always seem to cause us so much concern and worry. Everything that happens to us is offering us an opportunity to learn some particular lesson, everyone who comes into our life has some particular reason for being here, some particular message for us.

And when we realise all this, we have a very different perspective on what happens to us and the people with whom we come into contact as we continue on this, our earthly journey, Spiritual beings, having a physical experience for the duration of this life-time only, in order to increase our own Spiritual consciousness and to raise the collective Spiritual consciousness of all humanity.

Yeshua told us: *'Be passersby'.*   In other words, we are only passing through on this earth plane, only travellers on our long walk-about across eternity. This earth plane is simply a bridge between dimensions, and when we see it as such, we do not get attached to what this world offers us, because we see everything as temporary and passing. Life goes on in a continuous flow, constantly changing, and it is our resistance to impermanence that causes us most of our pain and suffering. The dimensions beyond this earth dimension are those on which we need to keep focused, as they are the reality, this dimension being only temporary and transitory. The two biggest events of our physical lives, birth and death, occur only on this physical earth plane, again, part of all that is transitory and impermanent.

We are here to show love. Unconditional love. Love without attachments.

In the Gospel of Thomas, Logion 95 we read:

"Yeshua said: / 'If you have money, / do not lend it with interest, / but give it to the one / who will never pay you back.' "

Meaning that to show real love, unconditional love, love with no conditions attached, is to expect nothing in return. And when we give love unconditionally, we are free from expectations of any outcome. We are disinterested in the outcome, not in a way that shows indifference or apathy, but in a way that shows that our heart is completely open, completely transformed by unconditional love, expecting nothing in return.

Every single person who enters our life does so for a purpose. Every single thing that happens to us happens for a purpose. There is no such thing as a chance happening or chance meeting. There is no such thing as co-incidence. There is only what we call synchronicity. And synchronicity is simply everything happening in divine timing. Synchronicity is the result of Unity Consciousness, where we live in the Oneness, and where, as a result of living in the Oneness, everything flows harmoniously in divine timing.

Furthermore, it's not the getting there that is important. It's what you encounter and experience along the way that matters. It's not the end result that is important. It's the journey towards that end result that matters. We seem to spend so much of our precious time chasing after this and that until we get it! But, in doing so, we miss so much along the way! Our greatest moments are indeed those when we are still!! Not running or chasing around after our own tails, going nowhere!

Smell the coffee! Smell the roses! Admire the field of daffodils, watch the sun sink down over the horizon! As Celie says, in *'The Color Purple',* Alice Walker's beautiful novel, *'It pisses God off if you walk by the color purple in a field somewhere and don't notice it.'*

The Gospel of Thomas tells us:

"Yeshua said: A man cannot ride two horses / nor bend two bows. / A servant cannot serve two masters, / for he will honour one and disdain the other.' "

In other words, we cannot neglect our Spiritual body! We cannot deprive our Spiritual body of attention and care, and give as our excuse that we were looking after our physical body. We cannot even give them both equal care, attention and nurturing. We must give our Spiritual body more care than our physical body demands of us, simply because the Spiritual body is the real us, the infinite, immortal, unlimited us, while the physical body is temporary, destined to decompose and decay anyway!

The message is clear! We must nurture our Spiritual body! We are in this world, not of this world, and so we must not allow ourselves to become attached to the transient, material things of this world! They are the false, the wrong master!

CHAPTER 4:

Death and Birth

We have just seen in the previous chapters that we are all energy, constantly changing energy form, all the while remaining within the Great Universal God Energy, the Oneness, outside of which nothing and no one can have any possible chance of existence, because that is the energy source, the life source, the power source for the entirety of creation.

We saw too, how each and every one of us is a Spiritual being, a Spiritual being having a temporary physical experience for the duration of this life-time. We are Spiritual pilgrims, Spiritual nomads, inter-galactic travellers, travelling beyond the barriers of space and time through all eternity and infinity.

For most people, fear is inherent in the word death. We are afraid of dying and death. We are afraid of separation from our loved ones. And mostly, many people are afraid of nothingness, that they will just cease to be.

But in reality, there is actually no such thing as death or birth, in the way in which we think about them. In the higher vibration energy frequencies, birth and death do not exist. It is only here, on this dense earth energy vibration dimension that the notions of birth and death exist. And that is all they are! A notion! An idea in our heads!

Let us look at this more deeply.

Each time we re-incarnate and return to this earth dimension in the energy form of a physical body, we call this our *'birth'* and we celebrate our *'birthday'* every year with excitement and joy. Then when we come to exit each incarnation, we call this *'death'*. And those who remain behind us remember us on the *'anniversary'* of our *'death'*.

But! We have seen that this world is not our permanent abode. We are merely passing through on one of our long walk-abouts across the fathomless stretch of infinity and eternity.

Each time we leave the higher vibrational levels and come back to earth, we are simply starting a new adventure. But we are leaving our natural existence, our real home, where we really belong, in the higher vibrational frequency energy levels. Should we not be calling this our *'death'* then, in the sense that we are *'dying'* to our real home, the Light, and entering a lower, more dense energy vibration level where we exist mostly on the lower physical level with all its incumbent entourage of whatever life throws at us? That sure sounds like a *'death'* to me!

Then, when we exit this physical life, are we not releasing ourselves from this physical world of dense matter and returning to our natural home in the higher vibrational frequencies? That sure sounds like a *'birth'* to me, in the sense that we are being *'reborn'* into the Light from whence we came in the first place!

William Wordsworth, 1770-1850, probably the best known of the Romantic poets, explains in his *'Ode to Immortality'*:

' Our birth is but a sleep and a forgetting. Our soul that rises with us, our life's star, hath had elsewhere its setting, and cometh from

afar, not in entire nakedness, but trailing clouds of glory do we come from God who is our home.'

The ***forgetting*** that accompanies what we call ***birth***, the separation we see between ourselves and our true nature, forgetting who and what we truly are, - that is what death really is. Through the process that we see as ***birth***, we are actually ***dying*** to our real nature, and through the process of what we call ***death***, we are actually being ***re-born*** into our true and eternal nature.

Look at it like this. The little grubs at the bottom of the pond can see the light up at the top, beyond the surface of the water. Then one day, one little grub decides to try and climb up towards the light and see what is going on. So up the blade of grass he starts to climb, his other friends down below him cheering and willing him on. Then he reaches the surface and breaks through. Suddenly his energy form changes from that of a little grub into a beautiful dragonfly. He has broken through the surface and now, as a dragonfly, can no longer go back into the water. So he flaps his wings and flies off into the light, knowing that his friends are coming after him. His friends do not mourn him as **'*dead'*,** they see he has metamorphosed into a higher vibrational being and has gone off into a wonderful, exciting new form of existence. And they know they too are about to follow. And they are so excited! So looking forward to it!

This is certainly not what we can call the **'*death'*** of the little grub! In fact it is definitely a **'*birth'*** into a much brighter, higher existence! He has got himself out of the darkness of the murky waters into the brightness of the light.

And of course, the caterpillar and the butterfly! We do not consider that the transition of the caterpillar to a butterfly is an any way a '*death*'!

So, have we got those terms '*birth*' and '*death*' the wrong way round? It certainly seems like it! Surely we experience '*death*' first, leaving our permanent home, '*dying*' to that higher existence level of energy, and then being '*born*' back into that higher level again when we complete our journey through this life-time?

The reason why we see birth and death as we do is because we are simply seeing the physical part of us. But that is only the temporary aspect! We see birth as celebratory, death as sorrowful and uninviting.

And the reason why so many people continue to fear death is because of what they have been led to believe happens when we pass over. Contrary to what we have been led to believe and what has been instilled into us from our early years, death is not something to be feared or to worry about.

So what happens when we pass back to the higher Spiritual energy levels, or as we put it, when we '*die*'?

Well, first of all, we do not '*die*' in the conventional meaning and understanding of that term. There is no such thing as '*death*'. Fact!

We saw earlier on how we are all energy. And we saw how energy never dies. It simply changes form. So, we, as energy, never '*die*', we simply change energy form. It is just our physical body that will decay through time. But we are NOT just that physical body, as we have seen earlier. We are a Spiritual body! And our Spiritual body is immortal.

The actual process of what we call death, which is the process of transitioning to a higher consciousness level, to a state of greater awareness, is just a process of change in the energetic field. When it comes the time for our exit from this earthly dimension, the physical life we have experienced comes to an end when we take our last breath as a physical being. Spirit is breath, breath is Spirit. Breath is the transmitter of Spirit. So our Spirit, what we really are, leaves our physical shell and returns to the higher vibration frequency levels. Our Spirit gravitates back toward the Light which beckons us. We simply leave our physical body behind and depart with our soul energy to one of the associated energy levels on the higher planes of energy.

This departure from our physical body is heralded by a washing of the auric field, a clearance, and an opening of the chakras. The three lower chakras begin to dissolve, and as they dissolve, they transmute into beautiful opalescent clouds, similar to mother-of-pearl, and waft gently off, bringing an opalescent quality to the hands, the face and the skin. The energy is then flushed right up through the higher chakras to the crown chakra, which is the direct portal into other dimensions. As this flushing out takes place, all blockages are removed and the person's entire life-time flashes before them, with a now clear remembering of what and who we truly are, and an integration into and with the Higher Self. We are now in the vastness and the lightness of our true being, where our senses are expanded and heightened in the magnificence of our realization of what we truly are in the *Oneness* of *All That Is*.

No one stops us or asks us where do we think we are going! Our soul, that immortal part of us, automatically gravitates towards the level in the higher vibration frequency energy levels for which we have prepared ourselves in this life-time. No-one questions us about how much money we have given to charity, how many good deeds we have done, how many people we have helped. To be honest, it is of no interest to anyone in the Spiritual realms! The only criteria applied is what level of soul awareness, what level of Spiritual consciousness have you managed to get yourself to? That means, very simply, what is your understanding of God, Oneness and life, and the whole concept of energy, and how aware are you that you are a Spiritual immortal being? Your soul automatically knows where to go. After all, you have made this journey many times before and you will do so many times again.

There is no judgement, either by yourself, by some sort of male punishing God, or by any other being. There is no hell, no purgatory, no sort of punishment awaiting us. Such ideas have been instilled deeply into us by controlling religions, using fear and guilt to exert control over us and keep us in subservience, to keep us dependent on religious institutions, on those who have set themselves up as the sole intermediaries between us and this dreaded God in the sky, a dreaded God who does not even exist!

It's all fake news!

In the Gospel of Mary of Magdala, unlike the canonical gospels adapted by the early Roman Christian Church in order to instil fear into us, God is not portrayed as a revengeful or punishing ruler or judge, but is simply referred to as the Good. Nor is God called Father, for gender, sexuality, and the social roles ascribed to them are part of this lower material earth realm, part of the thinking on this dense earth dimension.

You have a life review, where you will see how you performed this time around, and how well you learned the lessons you came here to learn. Any hurt you caused to any other person, you will now feel as they felt, and it will bring you to your knees. On the other hand, any kindness you showed to any other form of life, you will also feel how that person felt, and you will rejoice.

Your loved ones who have already passed back to Spirit before you, are waiting to welcome you home, and to shower you with congratulations on how you performed this time around. They have been alongside you the whole journey, just on different vibration energy frequency levels. There has never been any separation. There can never, ever be any separation. We are all **One**!

When you pass over, no one forces you to do anything. You have always got a choice. You can choose how you wish to continue on your own Spiritual evolutionary path, and whether or not you may wish to return to the earth vibration. If your loved ones are on a higher vibrational frequency level than where you find yourself at first when you pass over, you will still be able to connect with them. You cannot access their higher vibrational level, as you have not yet gained access to that higher level, but they can always descend to your level in order to facilitate a meeting.

'Sleep in peace' is a common prayer at any funeral. But one thing you will certainly not be doing is sleeping! Yes, you will be at peace, but not sleeping! Your evolutionary Spiritual progress continues. We never stop learning and advancing up the higher

vibrational Spiritual energy levels. It's a long way right to the top, to the ultimate vibration energy level, so we keep going.

You have the choice to return to this dense earth dimension, to fast-track your soul development. We often wonder why anyone would choose to come back here, or worse still, choose a life of particular suffering and hardship, when they could remain in the higher Spiritual frequencies. Well, I have just given you the answer! Those who choose a life of hardship and suffering are fast-tracking! They will achieve much more than someone who takes it much more slowly and has life after life of ease and comfort. Remember! There is no such thing as time in the higher vibration energy levels. We are in no hurry! We have all eternity for all of this! What's the hurry?

If you do decide to return, then you plan your own life in the minutest detail for your next time around. Nothing is left to chance, for there is no such thing! You choose your own parents, those who will best help you learn the lessons which you yourself have chosen to learn.

And so you return. Life unfolds exactly as you yourself planned it. You know only your own life-plan, and not the life-plan of anyone else. So, as we will see in later chapters, we can never judge anyone, simply because we do not know enough about their life-plan to enable us to see where they are coming from, and we cannot control any one else's life-plan, as that is their life-plan, not ours, so we just have to mind our own business, literally, and look after our own life-plan, and only our own life-plan.

So, to repeat, there is no need to fear death, because death does not even exist! There is no need to fear a punishing God when we pass over because a punishing God does not exist either! So you see, we can spend a lot of our life-time worrying and fretting over what does not actually exist! Daft or what?

And while mourning and grieving for our loved ones who have passed over is perfectly normal and understandable, we should remember that they have completed their life mission and have passed on to another, higher, more elevated level of existence, that which they have earned for themselves in this life-time. It is a time for great rejoicing and celebration, as they make their transition into one or other of the multiple energy levels in the higher dimensions of existence. They have completed and fulfilled their role in this dimension, and they now take on a different role or job in the higher vibration energy levels in order to continue on their soul evolutionary path.

Yes, when a loved one passes on, we experience all sorts of emotions, from anger, grief, confusion to overwhelming despair and a sense of being deserted and left behind. But we will be with our loved ones again in a glorious reunion, when the veil will be lifted from our eyes and we will see exactly the role that person chose to play in our life. Our loved ones are happy where they are, in an environment of unconditional love and light, just on a higher energy level than we who are left behind on this earth plane. We should be grateful for having had them in our life on this energy level, and know that we will be together again in a higher, brighter, happier dimension, where there is no pain, unhappiness or sorrow.

So there can be no such thing as **death** for us, as we are not merely physical bodies, but Spiritual beings. Jesus himself explains in the Gospel of Mary of Magdala:

"They asked him: 'Will matter then be utterly destroyed or not?'/ The Saviour replied: 'They will dissolve again into their own proper root. For the nature of matter is dissolved into what belongs to its nature.' " (Gospel of Mary of Magdala, page 5.)

Jesus here teaches us that when we come to pass back to the higher Spiritual realms at the end of our physical life, then our physical human body dissolves back again into the elements out of which it came; only the Spiritual soul is immortal and lives forever. We are Spiritual beings, made in the image of God, and we will overcome the worldly attachments that lead to suffering and death, we will transcend all things appertaining to this physical world dimension. Not only are we dust and will return to dust, as with our physical body, but we are also Light and will return to Light, as in our real Divine Essence.

The greatest fear many people have about death is that it is the annihilation, the ending of the personal self, that we will just fade into nothingness. But as we have seen earlier, there is no such thing as the personal self and there never ever has been such a thing as the personal self. Nothing, absolutely nothing exists in, of or by itself. So how can we fret and worry and fear something which has never ever been in existence? This thinking just does not make sense! Each one of us is a composite, an integral unique component of the **Great Universal God Energy**, and as such, we are eternal, unlimited, unending. We will always be in existence within this Great Universal God Energy, simply because that is what we are!

Death is just a transitioning from one state of consciousness to another. In believing that **death** is the end, we truly are our own worst enemies!

We are simply transitioning back again peacefully from this dense energy vibration of Planet Earth into the higher Spiritual energy vibration levels, where there is no judgement, no punishment, no pain, no sorrow, only unconditional love, peace and joy, in the **Oneness** of **All That Is**, in the Great Universal God Consciousness, in the Great Universal God Energy, where we have all always been, but now simply transitioning to a higher, more glorious level within that all-encompassing Universal Energy.

Happy days!

CHAPTER 5:

Reality versus illusion

Nothing is ever as it seems! Fact!

For example, we look at a person in front of us. We see the physical body and we usually form an opinion on what we see. But that physical body is **NOT** that person! That person's true identity is the bright shining Spiritual Light beyond the physical body.

The physical body is the illusion, the Spiritual Light of the person is the reality. But we do not see it! We do not acknowledge it! Simply because we are looking at everything from the perspective of this earth energy dimension, this earth energy vibration frequency, which is where we reside for this life-time.

Herein lies the core of one of our biggest problems, one of our greatest barriers to having a peaceful, joyful life! We see everything as happening to just our physical body. And why? Because that is the very limited way in which we continue to see ourselves!

But to repeat! We are not just a physical body! And what is done to the physical body cannot affect our Spiritual body, the real part of us, the part that will go on and on for ever, while the physical body decays and is discarded, of no further use to us.

This world is not our real home. Nor is it our permanent home. We are here for just a short-term sojourn, on a mission. But we give too much attention to what this world can give us, rather than paying attention to our Spiritual home. We are confusing the reality with the illusion! We are **in this world** right now, but we are not **of this world**.

So how do we define and understand reality?

Reality is a relative state of existence. Relative to what? Relative to other states of existence. I appear as I am here on this earth plane **ONLY** on this earth plane. In the other vibration levels on which I appear, I am different from I am here. I am observed in my true Spiritual essence by beings from higher vibration energy frequencies. They see us in our Spiritual form, not as we appear on this earth frequency, in our physical bodies. They do not see us committing what we call sin, for example, nor are they watching us performing any of our normal bodily functions. Such acts as these only exist on this earth energy frequency, and do not even register on the radar of beings from higher dimensions.

So, reality is an experience at a particular energetic energy level, and reality for each one of us depends on what level of energy frequency we are on at any given stage in our soul evolutionary process. Whatever energy frequency we are on, reality for us is determined by that particular energy vibration.

In his last incarnation as a human being in a physical body on the energetic frequency of Planet Earth, Jesus was experiencing life on a particular Essenic level, the Essenes being the secretive Jewish sect of which he was a member. Yes, Jesus was trying to bring about a cultural change, to introduce a new concept of the world and change the common mind-set. That mind-set that was steeped in religious superstition and belief in a punishing, male God who sought vengeance and demanded blood sacrifices and penance as appeasement.

This life-time is only a dream! It is not real in the sense that it has any sort of permanency! We are asleep in this life in the sense that we are lacking in awareness of the higher energy vibration frequencies that surround us on all sides. And asleep in the sense that we do not know what anyone else's life plan is, or what lessons they have chosen to learn this time around. And that is why we cannot judge anyone, simply because we do not know from where anyone is coming. We simply do not know enough of anyone's story to be in a position to form a valid or trustworthy opinion.

Nothing is ever as it seems!

William Wordsworth, probably the best-known of the early 19th Century Romantic poets, could tell us: *'Our birth is but a sleep and a forgetting'*.

And it is time to waken up from that dream and that sleep and enter reality! Our thoughts create a dream-like world of appearance and deception, a charade we all mistake for reality. But being in reality, which is living in the knowledge and in the awareness that this physical world is not what life is all about, releases us into the ever abundant, peaceful and joyous flow of life now.

The sense of isolation that comes from seeing ourselves as separate from the Oneness of life leaves us feeling cut off and alone within the great pantomime, the great charade acting-out stage performance called *'**my life**'*. Because that's all it is! A pantomime! A charade! A stage performance!

And in this illusion, this pantomime we call life, we are trading our inner abundant truth and reality, the One undivided and omni-present source of all, for the limited thought identity of our ego. Death, sin and loss are all illusions! They only exist on this dense earth energy vibration level! They do not feature in any way, shape or form on any other vibration frequency.

In the Gospel of Mary of Magdala, we read:

"Peter asks: 'What is the sin of the world?' / The Saviour responds: ' There is no such thing as sin.'

We are all pure Spiritual light, bathed in innocence, not in the sense of being gullible or naive, but in the sense of being pure unconditional love, uncontaminated by any sort of negativity. Shakespeare, in *'Macbeth'* over 400 years ago, put life into perspective for us:

'Tomorrow, and tomorrow and tomorrow / Creeps in this petty pace from day to day, / To the last syllable of recorded time; /And all our yesterdays have lighted fools / The way to dusty death. Out, out, brief candle! / Life's but a walking shadow, a poor player / That struts and frets his hour upon the stage, / And then is heard no more. It is a tale / Told by an idiot, full of sound and fury, / Signifying nothing.'

So, reality as we know it is simply just a relative experience. Reality as we experience it here on this dense earth energy frequency is not the same reality as is experienced by beings on other energy vibration levels.

And the only way we can measure our reality here on this earth vibration level, in the past, present and future, is through the concept of time, which is the subject of our next chapter.

What we see as reality, on this earth dimension, is merely an illusion!

Absolute reality is the Oneness of everything. We are all one and the same. We are all the same source manifesting as everything. We are that reality which transcends all conceptual understanding. To say '*I am*' is the only thing which cannot be disputed, the only thing that is real on all the various energy frequency levels.

CHAPTER 6:

Time is non-existent

Time is a demarcating factor solely for this earth vibration energy frequency. And time, even in this earth vibration frequency, differs depending on where exactly you happen to be on Planet Earth. For example, the further east you travel, the further ahead you are in time than the rest of the world. Likewise, as you travel westwards, you gain in time. Then when you cross the International Date Line, you either gain or lose a whole day, again depending on the direction in which you are moving.

 In just the same way as we saw in the previous chapter that life is an experience at a particular energetic level, so too, time is also experiential. Time is relative and flexible and, according to Albert Einstein himself, time, *"the dividing line between past, present, and future is an illusion"*. Planet Earth is enveloped in a time warp, a time warp which plays a vital part in our soul evolution and the raising of the collective Spiritual consciousness of all humanity.

Time divides all our experiences up into the past, present and future, for the simple purpose of affording humanity the time needed to learn the lessons we need to learn in order to progress upwards to the higher Spiritual energy frequencies and to eventually attain Mastery.

Those who have had a near-death experience mostly report having the feeling or sense that everything is happening at the one time, outside and beyond what we call our normal earthly dimension time flow. They describe a limitless experience of being aware of everything going on around them, everything happening simultaneously, with no demarcations of space or time. A sort of inter-galactic, inter-cosmic, in-the-one moment event!

Time apparently only exists on evolving planets, in order to assist its species in learning the lesson that we are all One in the total Oneness of the Great Universal God Energy, the lesson that all life is inter-connected, inter-twined and inter-dependent. It is only on evolving planets, such as earth, that there is separation or demarcation by time or space.

Time does not speed up as we grow older. In fact time has nothing to do with growing older. What speeds time up is not the number of earth years we clock up, but how we grow in consciousness, how we grow in increasing awareness of what and who we are, why we are here and our place in the infinity of creation. We are all beings of light, and the higher up the different energy levels in the Spirit world we reach, then the lighter we become. Time ceases to exist. That is our reality!

Basic physics teaches us that If you board a space rocket, and accelerate to the speed of light, time itself will slow down, until it eventually stops exactly at the speed of light. Likewise, when a planet is in a state of evolution, in what we call an Ascended State, towards a higher, lighter energy vibration frequency, time increasingly moves faster and towards a stop. Time ceases to exist. Simply because we are now in this heightened state of consciousness, and from this heightened state of consciousness, we are aware of the vastness of eternity and we feel the Oneness of All That Is, with everything happening simultaneously within that state of Oneness. In this expanded state of awareness, where time does not exist, we experience our multi-dimensionality, which is expressing and experiencing all states of consciousness and all places and all time at once, simultaneously, with no demarcations of time or space. There is no then or there, only here and now.

So, as we can see, time compresses as we experience our soul evolution, as we rise in Spiritual consciousness to higher, lighter forms of energy vibration levels of reality. And as we move higher up in our awareness of ourself and all of the Earth, time speeds by much more quickly for us, simply because we are now experiencing at a higher energy level than we were before.

And what is Awareness? What is Consciousness? What is total Consciousness?

Awareness is Consciousness. Consciousness is Oneness. And in that Oneness, we have a collective experience of everything. A collective experience of both past and present. We have connected to the Spirit worlds, where there is no concept of time or any sense of time passing, but where everything happens simultaneously.

Have you noticed how time seems to be speeding up recently? Perhaps you thought it was because you are getting older? But we have just seen that getting older has nothing to do with time passing. What then?

2012 is the answer! 2012, when the earth's energy vibration was raised by the alignment of all the planets in the solar system, a unique configuration which ended both a 260,000 year cosmic cycle and a 26,000 year cosmic cycle, ushering in a new cycle of raised vibration for Planet Earth and the human species.

And what happens when we raise our vibration? Time speeds up and moves towards a stop! So yes, time is, literally, speeding faster for us here on this earth frequency at this point.

Think of the universe as a hologram. A hologram is a special type of photograph or image made with a laser beam, in which the objects shown look solid, as if they are real, as if they have depth rather than appearing flat, and can appear as if they are moving. If you want to see a hologram, just look at your driving license, or your credit card or even money. However, simple holograms such as these, which exist to make forgery more difficult, aren't very impressive. You can see changes in colors and shapes when you move them back and forth, but they usually just look like sparkly pictures or streaks of color. When we think of the universe as a hologram, it is much more sophisticated. The universe is a vast and complex hologram, unlike an ordinary hologram. It is similar to watching a 3-D movie in a cinema. While we see the pictures as having height, width and depth, they in fact all originate from a flat 2-dimensional screen.

If you look at a hologram from different angles, you see objects from different perspectives, just like you would if you were looking at a real object. Some holograms even appear to move as you walk past them and as you look at them from different angles. Others change colors or include views of completely different objects, depending on how you look at them, like you can see on a paper note of money.

Holograms have another remarkable surprising quality. If you cut one in half, each half contains whole views of the entire holographic image. The same is true if you cut the hologram up into tiny pieces. Even a tiny fragment will still contain the whole picture. On top of that, if you make a hologram of a magnifying glass, the holographic version will magnify the other objects in the hologram, just like a real one.

Everything that there is, everything there ever was, and everything that there ever will be, is in the hologram of the universe. And again, if you cut the hologram into tiny pieces, all of the hologram continues to exist in each of those tiny pieces. Furthermore, as everything in the entirety of creation is inter-connected and inter-penetrating, so too everything in the hologram is inter-connected. And so, if you make a change in just one of the tiniest parts of any sector, that change is reflected throughout the entire pattern, as everything is contained in everything else. A little change in our life is mirrored everywhere in our world through the hologram of consciousness. And we can change everything with just our thoughts! That's the power we have to change our world!

William Blake, poet and mystic, 1757-1827 writes:

'To see a World in a Grain of Sand, / And a Heaven in a Wild Flower, / Hold Infinity in the palm of your hand, / And Eternity in an hour.'

Everything happens simultaneously in the higher Spiritual dimensions. The past is simply collective energetic vibrations which we can visit, as for example, through shamanic journeying. The future is in the hologram too, but we cannot experience what has yet to be, simply because of our reality on this earth plane, which is our relative state of existence, at this stage in our evolutionary process. Psychics and mediums, though, can tune into other vibration energy levels in order to pick up information.

In the Gospel of Thomas, Logion 91 we read:

"They said to him: / 'Tell us who you are / so that we may believe in you' / He answered them: / 'You search the face / of heaven and earth, / but you do not recognize / the one who is in your presence / and you do not know how to experience / the present moment.' "

What we are looking for is already here and now. There is nothing only the here and now. We experience the vastness of the present moment in all its dimension of time, space and beyond space-time. Time as we know it is non-existent. None other than the famous Albert Einstein himself concluded in his later years that the past, present, and future all exist simultaneously:

"Time is not at all what is seems. It does not flow in only one direction, and the future exists simultaneously with the past."

And:

"Time has no independent existence apart from the order of events by which we measure it."

Einstein believed there is only one single existence, with no real division between past and future. When his best friend Michele Besso passed away, Einstein wrote to Besso's family, explaining that even though Besso had now passed on to another form of existence before him, it did not matter, *"...for us physicists believe the separation between past, present, and future is only an illusion, although a convincing one."*

Everyone knows about Einstein's famous theory of relativity, proving that time is relative, and not absolute as Newton claimed. Take for example being in a very fast spaceship. The person travelling in the spaceship is travelling near the speed of light. The faster the spaceship travels, the slower time will pass for those inside the spaceship, relative to those still on the earth. If the spaceship were able to travel at the speed of light, time would cease completely, and those inside would be trapped in a timeless warp. Einstein's theories were discarded by other contemporary physicists, and even by those who followed him, the assumptions about the concept of time as we know it being very difficult to abandon.

So much for time, and it being non-existent. And what about space? Is there such a thing as empty space? When you are speaking to someone standing in front of you or right next to you, is the space between you empty? Or when you are lying on the beach looking up at the cloudless blue sky, is the space between you and the sky empty? Or when you are in an aeroplane, flying so many thousand feet above the earth, is the space outside all around you empty?

The truth is that space is full, rather than empty. There is no such thing as an empty space. And how do we work that one out? Well, as we have seen, cosmic energy, in all its multi-faceted forms, permeates everywhere. You only have to tune into NASA on U-Tube to hear the sounds all the various planets make as they revolve on their course. The music of the spheres! What Pythagoras taught over two thousand years ago! The planets emit various sounds as they continue on their path, sounds create vibrations and every vibration is energy. Likewise, when you are standing chatting to someone, your words are emitting sound vibrations out into the ether, and what we see as empty space is being filled with vibration energy, with energy waves.

And as we saw earlier, when we are not in manifestation in physical form on this earth energy frequency, we are still in existence. Where? We are still in existence as energy, waiting for the circumstances to be right for us to manifest again and again. We are taking up some of that which most people consider to be empty space. So there is no such thing as empty space! Energy permeates everywhere!

What we see as the universe, in all its vastness, is not just a single physical world, but a fragment of a much greater whole. And that much greater whole, in which absolutely everything is contained and to which everything is permanently connected, exists without any beginning or end, in the here and now, in this present moment of what we call time. Each moment we experience exists forever. And everything occurs simultaneously.

Finally, to end this chapter, how do you see time? Do you see time as linear? As cyclical? Do you see the year as linear or as cyclical? The week? The day?

Alan Wilson Watts, 1915-1973, was a British philosopher who interpreted and popularised Eastern philosophy for Western society, writing numerous books and articles on subjects important to Eastern and Western religion. Watts explored human consciousness in his book '*The Joyous Cosmology*' 1962 and in the essay '*The New Alchemy*', 1958.

And in Watts' learned and studied opinion:

"I have realized that the past and future are real illusions, that they exist in the present, which is what there is and all there is."

CHAPTER 7:

The Ego and the Higher Self

Our ego is our greatest enemy! It is our ego that continues to keep us in a state of separation. The ego is self, self-consciousness, self-righteousness. And that self-righteousness expresses itself as *'I'*, *'me'* and *mine'*, formed as a result of duality thinking. Duality thinking is believing that we are separate individuals, separate from the Oneness that is All. In order to live a productive and purposeful life, we need to be willing to change, evolve and relinquish the *'I'* through expansion of conscious awareness to the realisation of *'we'*, where we accept that we are one part of a greater whole. Ego, **E**diting **G**od **O**ut describes our separate existence and what we have become. It is the enemy of our Higher Self, which is us in our undiluted God Essence, us in the Oneness of the Great Universal God Energy.

And the difference in the ego and the Higher Self? The ego is the *false self*, as opposed to the Higher Self, which is the *true self*.

So relinquishing this false self, this ego, is hardly a sacrifice, because anything false is not real, it is only a gathering of thought in the mind. The ego is the sole source of all our fears, emptiness, unhappiness, stress and all things negative.

Ego identifies with form; with the outer manifestation of form in its various facets, which include physical forms, thought forms and emotional forms. When we identify completely with only physicality, thoughts and emotions, we are totally unaware of our

Divine connection, our connection to Divine Source. When we are ego motivated, we are confined, entrapped in our five physical senses. We live a sort of stagnant existence, never realising who we are, why we are here, or what we are here to do. So ego, therefore, can be explained as a lack of awareness of the connectedness with all other life-forms; a lack of awareness of the connection of each and every one of us with the whole, with the *'All That Is'.* When we exist in such a state of separateness, where we *E*dit *G*od *O*ut, we serve only the false self, and not the Higher Self, the false self being neither a recommendable nor a reputable master!

When we serve only the false self, the ego, we neglect, we deny, we negate the collective human consciousness. We are seeing only the surface, only what our five physical senses allow us to experience. We are failing to see the connectedness, the support mechanisms under the surface that maintain the whole universal energy which encompasses the whole of life, in every form, in the vast infinity of what we call creation. And ego is not just individual; ego is also collective. Collective in the ego of countries, nations, governments, religions and creeds. And in just the same way as ego serves the individual, it also serves the collective. In just the same as ego manifests for the individual, so too it also manifests for the collective. What ego does for the individual, ego also does for the collective.

And the result? The result is that when we transfer all this individual ego onto the collective world stage, we get this warring, fractured, decimated planet we now inhabit, where ego is running rampant, where ego is in control instead of being controlled. When we allow ourselves to live in jealousy, hatred, fear, judgement, desire for revenge, then we weaken our ability to recognise and use our full potential. In such a scenario, ego dominates, thrives and flourishes. The ego is the source of all human suffering. And why? Simply because ego, the vampire, is constantly sucking from humanity, rather than contributing to humanity. The twentieth century has seen two world wars, atomic bombs, biological weapons. All of this is resulting from fear and greed for power; humanity working from the false self, the ego, rather than from the Spiritual self, from the Higher Self. It is only when we develop and expand our conscious awareness that we learn to control the false ego.

What drives, what motivates, what sustains ego? Ego is driven, like everything else in life, by the desire, the urge, to preserve itself; to remain in existence; to save itself from annihilation; to save itself from being wiped out. If we choose to live in-Spirit, in an awareness of our Higher Self, the only alternative to living in-Ego, then ego becomes redundant, obsolete, defunct. And that is the last thing ego wants for itself! Ego is motivated by fear, greed and the desire for power and control. So how come this ego thing has so much control over us? How come we have allowed it to dominate our lives?

We allow ego to take over our lives because it makes us feel better about ourselves. It makes us feel we are superior to others. And, ironically, even though it continues to only operate on a temporary basis, it still manages to sustain itself. Ego sustains itself because it works so hard to sustain itself! It permeates every aspect of our lives. It oozes in everywhere. It lurks in all the corners. It disguises itself, unrecognisable, unidentifiable, under its many guises. And ego sustains itself through our human ignorance. When we live in-Ego, we live in an unawakened state, in a world of unawareness, in a world of unconsciousness. Unaware of what? Unconscious of what? Unaware of the connectedness of all life. Unconscious of the fact that we are all One, all One in the vast universal energy that sustains us. So what is the way out of our dilemma? We need to disentangle ourselves, separate ourselves from ego!

And how do we disentangle ourselves, how do we separate ourselves from ego? First, we need to remember who we really are! And then, in remembering who we really are, we re-align ourselves with our Spiritual self, our Divine Essence, our Higher Self, which brings peace, harmony, balance and the synchronistic flow of Universal Divine energy into our lives. Unless we know and understand the basic mechanics behind the workings of the ego, we cannot recognise it, and when we fail to recognise it, ego will trick us into identifying with it time and again. It takes us over, an imposter pretending to be our true nature, our true self.

And ego's main problem? Ego's main rival? Ego's main enemy? Ego's main obstacle, ego's main competitor is silence. And why? Because if ego allowed us to have silence in our lives, it would lose contact with us altogether. Then it would be exit ego! Ego gone; gone for good! Redundant! So ego operates a keep busy, busy, busy programme; a do, do, do programme; a go, go, go programme; a get, get, get programme.

Ego is that little voice inside of us, niggling away at us, gnawing away at us, urging us, forcing us to go, go, go; do, do, do; get, get, get. More, more, more! Ego tells us we are only this body, and as this physical body we are firmly rooted in earthly things; material possessions; worldly goods; worldly pleasures.

It is ego that tells us we are judged by the material possessions we manage to accumulate; the more we have, the more successful we will be in the eyes of others; the more we will be admired and emulated.

It is ego that tells us we need all this stuff we buy for self; self has to come first and foremost. The egoic mind identifies the person we are with the possessions we have. We lose our selves in our possessions. We become that huge house; we become that fabulous car; we become that expensive piece of exquisite jewellery. We are identified by others as the person with that huge house; that person with the fabulous car; that person with that exquisite jewellery. We have made it big! So having material possessions, ego tells us, gives us an identity. Yes! True! But a false identity! Material possessions rob us of our true identity; our true self! But ego triumphs yet again, and so we find ourselves in competition, in a battle, constantly preoccupied with achieving the most, the best, the biggest. No pressure there then! And how well those in the advertising industry can play on all this! Their job is simply to convince us that we need this or that product in order to enhance our lives; to simply convince us that the purchase of this or that will add something to our sense of self, in our own eyes and in the eyes of others. And so we buy it. Ego wins again!

It is ego that tells us we are separate individuals, in a competitive world, where only the fittest survive. And the result? The result of this separatist, individualistic programming by ego is competitiveness, cut-throat, man-eat-dog competitiveness;

competitiveness on a massively destructive scale, where there should be co-operation on a massively productive scale.

The work-place! Ego in its element! The epitome of egotism! The workplace has become a place where ego dominates. A soul-destroying, rather than a soul-enhancing place. A place where creativity is stifled rather than a place where the soul's creativity is encouraged, engendered, furthered. A place where natural talents and creativity are stifled, smothered, suffocated, instead of a place where they should be fostered, sponsored and guided to fruition. Before industrialisation, all in the name of so-called progress, individuals expressed themselves and their talents in creative masterpieces; coopers, iron-mongers, stone-masons and the like took pride, joy, satisfaction and fulfilment in their work. The creative soul flourished. And that is what we are meant to do! We are meant to create! We are meant to manifest the diverse creativity of the Divine. God Energy finds expression through us. That is why we are here! To give expression to the multi-facetedness of God's Creativity, and to experience that Creativity in all its diversity. And what exactly has industrial machinery added? Only a faster production line; more goods produced in less the time; more money! Well done ego! Consumerism's best friend!

The workplace has become a place where we are valued and assessed according to how productive we actually are in creating more money for our employers. And those of us who generate the more business and hence the more money, are those who will retain their job more easily. No pressure there either! The workplace should contribute to the overall enhancement and good of the community. It should not alienate or separate an individual from his own nature. Let's face it! Operating a machine, working on a production line, for example, does not exactly stimulate the creative part of the soul. In fact, all that has happened is that the soul has been taken out of work completely. Consumerism and increasingly higher production target levels are stifling creativity. Entrepreneurship cannot be conducive to all- round enhancement when it operates only at the expense, or to the detriment of everyone else. Machiavellian principles, where the good of the individual can be sacrificed for the good of the many has been allowed to dominate not only our political systems, but also our economic and industrial systems. And all this has come about because of the ego! Because the ego tells us that we are just this physical body; we are measured by the amount of material possessions we can accumulate; by how much money we can make; by how big a business empire we can build for ourselves. If we want to be noticed, if we want to be admired, we must be successful; successful in making money and gathering material possessions. Definitely no pressure!

So what else does this ego thing do for us? In what other ways does this ego show itself? Ego shows itself when we rant and rage against what is actually happening at any particular time. Road rage; having to get the last word in an argument; trying our best to get the outcome we think we know is best for us in any given situation; criticising; back-biting; belittling people; demanding thanks or praise; asserting our authority over others; dictating to others how they should live their lives or what they should do; making others out to be wrong and yourself right; all of these operate from us seeing ourselves as superior to others.

Probably the most frequent way in which the individual ego asserts itself is seen in our dependency on form for happiness. We crave satisfaction, fulfilment and happiness through acquiring more possessions; through acquiring the perfect body, the envy of all others. Like a child with a new toy, the novelty soon wears off, and we need another new material possession. We put our trust for happiness in transient, temporary form. We expect to find satisfaction in more, bigger, better, best. And then we wonder why relationships do not last! Relationships do not last because we demand more and more from them in order to satisfy our self-gratification, in order to feed our ego. We see everyone else through what they have materially; how they can best serve us in meeting our personal needs; how they look; how they dress; how much money they have. It's all about *me, my, mine.*

This ego will only disappear for good when we realise how limiting and evil it actually is. Ego is not our friend, but our enemy. Ego does not give, it takes. Ego promises everything, but delivers only very short-lived satisfaction and transient happiness. We only need to watch the daily television news programmes, read the daily newspapers to see the destruction, suffering and trauma ego inflicts upon the world. The bad news is that the unprecedented violence that humans are inflicting on other human beings and on other life-forms is testament to how rampant ego is in our world today. Fear, greed and desire for power, are powerful destructive weapons and it is these which feed the individual and collective ego. Failure to recognise our connectedness to the whole; failure to recognise that we are much more than just a physical body; failure to recognise that the good of the individual is best served through the good of the whole have all led us to this present brink of destruction.

And the good news? The good news is that once we recognise the ego for what it actually is, then we can become more aware of our thoughts and emotions that feed that ego. And then we can experience the shift from ego thinking to awareness; to awareness of a greater connectedness to all forms of life; to a greater power than us; to an awareness of who we truly are, and when we increase this awareness, this consciousness, then we will be able to destroy the ego for good. And then we will experience the joy, the peace, the fulfilment for real; the peace, the joy, the fulfilment that ego promised us, but because of its very nature, could not deliver.

Spirit or your own Higher Self is your reality, while thought identity or ego is the imposter. When we are ego motivated, we are trapped in our senses. We find ourselves at the mercy of what has been previously learned about who we are. Too many people live in this kind of stagnant existence, never realizing who they are, why they exist, or what they are here to do. And in that state of stagnant existence is where ego wants us to remain. In a state of duality, in a state of separation, in a state of limited awareness, where the ego is in control! But to our own detriment!

CHAPTER 8:

Go with the flow!

Consider the trees, how they bend and sway in the wind. They do not try to resist the wind, simply because they know there is no point in doing so! Observe the tree in the middle of the river. The water gushes all around it. The tree does not try and divert the flow of water or block it. It just remains fixed and allows the water to flow along. The birds eat just what they need to satisfy their hunger at any one time and leave the rest, because they know that when they are hungry again, food will materialise. There are lessons for us here!

Look how nature teaches us the lessons of patience and trust, and how everything is happening exactly as it should, for our own highest good. We live in an abundant universe, with plenty for all. The whole of creation is looked after by a master plan, a higher Intelligence, omniscient, omnipotent, omnipresent, in the most intricate design.

And what do we need to do? We just need to let go and let God. We need to trust in the universe to deliver! Simpy because that is what the universe does! The universe delivers!

The trees in autumn show us how lovely it is to let things go! There is beauty in letting go! But we hold on. We fight against the current. We resist change. We try and control the outcome. And in going after our own outcome, in trying to take control and force things to happen as we want them to happen, we prevent the universe from getting to us what is for our highest good. We interfere and block the flow of universal energy. We need to let the Great Universal Energy flow naturally, and not block it by getting attached to any particular outcome.

"Yeshua said: / 'Do not worry from morning to evening, / or from evening to morning, / about having clothes to wear.' " (Gospel of Thomas Logion 36)

That means, stop worrying! Worrying about anything, however small or great, shows you do not trust in the universe to deliver! Worry is based on fear, and fear is a sign of a lack of inner peace and confidence. Letting go of worry does not mean becoming indifferent or irresponsible. It just means realising that the outcome of our actions is always for our highest good.

Ignatius of Loyola wrote:

'In all things, perform your act as if everything depends on it alone; and in all things, act as if the outcome of everything you do depends on God alone.'

So send your request out there into the universe, and then leave it to the universe to deliver that or something better. When we allow the flow of life, when we end the struggle to become this or that, and begin placing our trust in the universe, we find an ease and lightness in everything we do. We also find that elusive better way of living, which the majority of humanity craves to find. And when we learn to go with the great universal flow, we have indeed awakened.

Life is an adventure! And when setting out on an adventure, you do not know what is going to happen! You just let it all unfold! You roll with the punches. You flow with the current. By going with the flow, you enjoy all aspects of life. You don't know what is going to happen, but you are open to whatever, embracing all with open arms.

Your life will never work whilst you remain in stress! And stress can only come from lack of trust in the universe, lack of trust that a Greater Intelligence has everything under control for our own highest good.

Just go with the flow. The path of least resistance and all that!

CHAPTER 9:

Mind your own business!

Each of us arrives back, yet again, in this earth dimension with our own unique blue-print for our earthly journey this time around. We have freely and willingly chosen the lessons we wish to learn in order to evolve our own immortal soul.

It is enough to be looking after our own life-plan without looking after and sticking our nose into everyone else's life-plan as well! Ironic, really, when we do not even know what that life-plan actually is!

If you want to live a peaceful, harmonious joyful life, then you have got to leave other people alone! If you are sticking your nose into other people's lives, then you are guaranteed that a peaceful, harmonious, joyful life will not be yours!

And that also means that you do not try and manipulate your children into doing what you want them to do. Each of them has his own unique path to follow, his own personal journey to make, his own lessons to learn. And you cannot learn those lessons for him!

Look at it this way. If your child comes home from school with a passage from Shakespeare to learn, would you try to learn it for him? Most definitely not! You can help him to learn it by, perhaps, saying it over and over again with him, but he must do the learning of it for himself. It is just the same with the lessons your child has chosen to learn in this life-time. They are his lessons, not yours, his life, not yours, his learning path, not yours. Just mind your own business! That is enough for you to be getting on with!

And if he wants to grow his hair until it is long enough for him to sit on it, cover his body with tattoos, and head off around the world with his back-pack and a guitar, then he has every right to do just that. You might not like it, but you have no right to prevent him from doing it. You just need to mind your own business!

Nor have you the right to re-live your life through your children by forcing them into the family business or into a particular professional career or business simply because you yourself are in this profession or business. Or to try and live the life through your children, the life that you never had. Imagine your son or daughter going to work in the family business every day just because you forced them into it! What kind of negative energy are they bringing into work with them? Certainly not the energy which is going to do anybody any good!

Taking on your children's problems and trying to solve them is doing no good for anyone. Not only do your children fail to learn the lessons they came here in the first place to learn, but you, well you just end up with shoulder and neck pains! Shoulder and neck pains from carrying other people! Everyone's a loser! If you continuously collect all the dirty socks and other dirty clothes lying across the floor of your children's bedrooms and put them in the laundry basket, then how are they ever going to learn to do all that for themselves, which one day they most certainly will have to do? If you continue to hand out cash every time it is asked for, because you want your children to have the same as everyone else, how are they going to learn to fend for themselves, which is something they will definitely one day have to do? You are not helping! In fact you are hindering them from learning what they need to learn!

And if you suffer from shoulder and neck pains, then just ask yourself, of all the worries and concerns you have, how many of them actually belong to you yourself? I would say probably very few or even none! They are all someone else's problems and worries! So let everyone else get on with their own lives and get on with learning the lessons they came here to learn! Very often the most difficult thing to do is to do nothing and say nothing. But that is exactly what you must do! Nothing!

And minding your own business also means not gossiping or stabbing someone in the back or trying to figure out what is going on inside anyone else's head. And you know what? Most of the time when we are involved in such negative activities, it is because we are trying to avoid looking at ourselves! What we see to criticise in others is often a reflection of what is going on in our own life!

Each one of us is responsible for our own life and only our own life. We are not responsible for anyone else's life. Nisargadatta Maharaj, an Indian sage born in Mumbai in 1897 wrote *"Those who know what is good for others are dangerous people"*.

So look after your own life! And only your own life! That's enough for you to be getting on with! Minding your own business, and only your own business guarantees you a life of inner peace and harmony.

So take a step back! Mind your own business and allow everyone else to get on with their own life!

CHAPTER 10:

KARMA

We have been brought up with two very distinctly different images of God. On the one hand we have been taught that God is a punishing God, so we had better behave ourselves, otherwise we will end up in hell, or if we are lucky, maybe just be punished with a temporary sojourn in that place beyond the sky somewhere called purgatory.

On the other hand we have been taught about this all-merciful God, who forgives all our misdemeanours and loves us, his children, unconditionally.

These two pictures cannot both be true! And the truth is that neither of them is true! What a relief!

We saw earlier that God is not any person and does not have a form. God is the Great Universal Energy, the Great Universal Consciousness, which incorporates us all, everything that is, that ever has been and that ever will be, and outside of which nothing and no-one can possibly have any sort of existence. God has no face, no hands, no mouth, no body of any description. And you will be waiting a long time after you go through those metaphorical pearly gates we have been told about into the Spiritual vibration energy frequencies before God comes to meet you! That is just not going to happen!

And when I say that God does not forgive, I know I am raising many eyebrows!

114

But look at it this way. Let me repeat that! God does not forgive! And why does God not forgive? God does not forgive simply because there is nothing for God to forgive! And why is there nothing for God to forgive? There is nothing for God to forgive simply because Karma takes care of everything! That's it in a nutshell! Fact!

Karma is not a punishment. Karma is simply a balancing, a balancing of our not-so-good deeds with our good deeds. Karma applies to everyone, absolutely everyone, no-one escapes. Karma trundles down through life-time after life-time, keeping us on the wheel of reincarnation until we have managed to pay back our Karma, to balance our Spiritual record sheet.

Sometimes we may say that such and such a person never gets caught, he gets away with everything. Well, the truth is that no-one, absolutely no-one, gets away with anything, never mind getting away with everything. All must be balanced in our own personal Spiritual accounts ledger, and paid back, either in this life-time or in a future life-time. There is no escape for any of us! Fact!

The basic premise of Karma is that what we give out, we get back. That's one of the indisputable, the irrefutable, the irrevocable Spiritual laws of the Universe! And that Universal Law applies to us all! There are no exceptions to that rule!

Every word, every thought, every action goes out from us in the form of an energy vibration frequency, and joins the Great Universal Energy, attracting the same type of energy vibration frequency back to us, just like a magnet does. Everything in energy vibration frequencies is cyclical, there are no straight lines, all moving and swirling in cyclical motion. At some stage what we put out must come back to us, it has nowhere else to go! Just like a boomerang! It will come back and slap us in the face! Ouch! That hurt!

Once we put a vibration out there in the form of our words, our thoughts, our actions, we cannot stop it, we cannot delete it, because remember, energy cannot be ended, it cannot be killed.

But, it can be changed! It can be transmuted! And we are in control! We are able to transmute or change any negative, destructive energy we have sent out there!

And just how do we manage to do that?

Well, think of it this way. When you go into a dark room, how do you get rid of the dark? Sweep it all up into a bag and throw it out? Hardly!

You get rid of the dark very simply, by turning on the light switch! The dark has not gone away anywhere, it is still there, because when you turn the switch off again, the dark is still there! You have simply transmuted it into the light!

In the same way, you too can transmute any vibrational negative energy you send out. Say you are envious and jealous of someone. What have you just done? You have just sent out a negative vibrational energy, which will return to you at some stage. That is a heavy, cumbersome energy, and will trundle along, at some point returning to you with more of the same which it has gathered up along the way. In the meantime, you realise that you have done wrong, you regret having done that, and you now send out

116

thoughts of love and light to that same person. Now what have you done? You have now sent out a lighter, faster energy, which will eventually overtake the slower, heavier, more cumbersome energy you sent out previously. This lighter, faster energy will transmute the darker energy, returning to you as positive, light energy. That nasty boomerang has been avoided! Phew!

Yes, you can always change or transmute the energy you send out! You are in control! You are in control of what comes back to you!

Picture this. Morning rush hour. You are about to start the daily run to school. The toast has burned. The baby has just deposited something in its nappy, again! Another youngster has just spilled egg on his school uniform. Another cannot find her school bag! The other two are fighting! And you? You are on the extreme edge of a nervous break-down! In an over-the-top flap! If you allow yourself to carry on like this and get into that car and start driving, then what will happen?

It's all about energy again! It's always about energy!

If you start to drive in your present condition, where you are sending out those over-the-top frazzled thoughts and feelings, then you are going to attract all the other over-the-top frazzled drivers and people out there, because, as we have just seen, energy attracts and magnetises similar energy back to itself. At the worst, there is going to be an accident. So what can you do to save this situation?

You can change your energy! You cannot change anyone else's energy, you can only change your own. And then when you have changed your own, in this case to a calm quiet energy, sending out love and light to everyone, then you will attract other calm, love and light senders into your energy field. All those other over-the-top frazzled energy senders will no longer be attracted to you and instead go after all the other over-the-top frazzled energy senders! The traffic lights will turn green for you, other drivers will let you into the traffic flow, and you will arrive at school on time! And most importantly, you will have avoided a nervous melt-down!

Simple, really!

All you have to do is calm down, take a few deep breaths, change your thoughts and send out a different energy. Everyone's a winner!

So you see, if you want to live in joy, harmony and peace, then you must take control of your thoughts! If you send out thoughts of envy, greed, hatred, then that is what you will get back! If you send out thoughts of love, harmony and peace, then again, that is what you will get back.

You are in control! You are in control of the energy you send out there in your thoughts and words, and which then in turn attracts like energy back to you. You are the creator of your own thought forms. And when you understand and accept that what you set in motion through your own thought-forms will work with you and gain vitality as it joins the mass thought-forms already out there, for good or bad, then you will be much more cautious and careful. You will realise that it does not serve you in any way whatsoever to be jealous, angry, spiteful or whatever, because when you give those negative energy vibrations life by creating them in the first place through your thought-forms, they come back to haunt you, in order for you to actually experience the power and the effects of your own creative force. What you yourself set in motion is what you yourself will experience.

You are in control of whether you go through life seeing yourself as a victim, with the poor-me attitude, everyone's against me, it's not fair, buffetted about from post to pillar, or whether you go through life with inner peace, joy and harmony.

Remember! The world does not come *at* you, but *from* you!

Are you seeing the glass as half-full or half-empty? It's up to you! It's always up to you!

And karma does not just apply to individuals. There is also collective karma, for communities and nations.

Our karma for destruction of nature and the human race is indeed great. We have destroyed and wreaked havoc not only on human lives, but also, as we saw in an earlier chapter, on nature and the earth.

We are responsible for the governments we vote into power. Almost all of earth's population desire and long for peace. But there is still that proportion who wish to control, through war and threats.

CHAPTER 11:

Enough is enough!

What we have, what we need and what we want are all different! And of course, ironically, the more we have the more we want. We do indeed tend to live life with the view that more is better. On the other hand, we have the old saying, less is more.

We live in an affluent society, in an abundant universe, where there is more than enough for everyone. So how come so many people in our world have nothing, while others have so much they just don't know what to do with it all?

The answer lies in the fact that we are failing to see ourselves as all **One.** We are seeing instead the *self*, and the need to satisfy the self, no matter what. We see life as a rat-race, where only the strongest survive and where our success is marked by the amount of wealth we can accumulate, by the amount of titles we can gather and the amount of power we can wield.

But the truth is, we cannot buy happiness, good health or inner peace, no matter how much wealth we are able to accumulate, no matter how many material possessions we are able to gather. Happiness cannot come from transitory material possessions. Wanting less, being satisfied with what you already have, and taking time to appreciate and enjoy it all is a major key to happiness and inner peace. Not struggling to accumulate more and more! What are you actually going to do with all this stuff you have gathered?

It is an inner yearning that compels us to continue to gather material possessions. When we continue to attempt to satisfy our inner cravings by getting more and more material possessions, all we are doing is giving ourselves a quick fix, temporary gratification. We are misreading the signals! The yearning within us is not for temporary gratification through material possessions. The yearning within us is our soul crying out to be fed, to be nurtured, to be acknowledged. Our problem is a Spiritual problem, not an economic problem, and so only a Spiritual solution will work!

It is the same with the problems in the world right now. The problems are neither political nor economic. They are Spiritual, stemming from the fact that we are failing to see each other as the Divine Essence each one of us really is. If we could just see the Divine Light within each of us, then we would not judge, we would not condemn, we would not hate, or we would not hold feelings of envy or greed. And we would not gather more than we need at the expense of others having to go without. So because the problem is a Spiritual one, then only a Spiritual solution can be applied.

Sharing is the key, not owning. Sharing in a world where we are all **One**. I am you and you are me. What I do to you, I do to myself. I cannot have more than I need, when you are lacking.

In this fast moving world of instant gratification, where we expect to get everything instantly, - instant communication, instant everything, including even instant porridge, instant coffee, a quick fix for this, a quick fix for that, we are so busy going, going, going, doing, doing, doing, getting, getting, getting, that we don't notice or appreciate all that is for free all around us. We just do not appreciate what we have at this moment in time, but instead we are constantly looking ahead and planning what we are going to get or do next. Planning for a future which does not exist, because when tomorrow or next week or next year comes, it is still the present. And the present is the only place we can ever be. There is nowhere else! But because we are so busy, busy, busy, we fail to recognise that all we have is the present, all we have is this present moment in time.

So stop and smell the roses! Smell the coffee! Take time to stop and admire the abundant beauty all around us!

And give your house a good clear out! De-cluttering your house is de-cluttering your mind. Feel the weight fall from your shoulders! The weight of being weighed down with too much material possessions! Remember, we are Spiritual beings! And when we pass on after this life-time to our next level of existence, we will take no material possessions with us.

And don't forget! Everything must be kept in circulation, especially money. What you hoard, you will lose!

So work out what is really important to you. A quick, temporary, transitory, fleeting gratification of more material possessions or more money, or a deeper Spiritual satisfaction that comes from being detached from the things of this dense earth energy vibration, knowing they will all decay, while our souls will continue on their immortal journey?

Think of a young child on Christmas morning. The excitement of those new toys! An excitement that has been building up for months! But by lunch time what has happened? The novelty has worn off, and other children's presents are of more interest. And indeed, even the boxes and the wrappings are now more enticing!

William Wordsworth 1770-1850, one of the first of the 'Romantic' poets, summed it all up for us in *'The World is too much with us'*:

'The world is too much with us; late and soon / Getting and spending, we lay waste our powers; / Little we see in Nature that is ours; / We have given out hearts away, a sordid boon! / This sea that bares her bosom to the moon; / The winds that will be howling at all hours, / And are up-gathered now like sleeping floweres; / For this, for everything, - we are out of tune. / It moves is not!'

And the late 19th Century poet Thomas Hardy wrote: *'Everything glowed with a gleam, / Yet we were looking away'.*

In other words, because we are surrounding ourselves and bolstering ourselves up with non-life-sustaining material possessions, we have lost touch with our own inner being, we have lost touch with what is important to us, we have lost the ability to appreciate what we already have and the beauty that lies around us.

Enough is enough!

CHAPTER 12:

Being true to yourself

'You will know the truth and the truth will set you free.' (John 8:32)

'If you know the truth, the truth shall make you free.' (Gospel of Philip, Plate 132)

'While hidden, truth is like ignorance: it keeps to itself. But when it is revealed, it is recognized and glorified, for it is far more powerful than ignorance and error. It brings freedom........ignorance is slavery. Knowledge is freedom. When we recognize the truth, we raise its fruits in ourselves. When we unite with truth, it shares its fulness with us.' (Gospel of Philip, Plate 132)

These words have been repeated time and time again right down through history from the bible to modern-day poets.

Unless you are true to yourself, then you cannot be true to anyone else. But what does being true to yourself actually mean?

First and foremost, being true to yourself means gaining true self-knowledge. True self-knowledge is being aware of and being conscious of the whole of you, all that you are, and not just you in your physical identity.

True self-knowledge means knowing that you are part of a Greater Intelligence, and that you yourself are known to that Greater Intelligence. Within that Greater Intelligence, you are a unique expression of creation, an individualised expression of life, an individualised expression of consciousness.

And being true to yourself, as that unique expression of life, means living your life as the person you really want to be, because you yourself want to be that person, and not pretending to be someone else just in order to please, to fit into society, or to gain favour or acceptance.

It means not taking on a career or job simply because your parents are in that walk of life and expect you to follow in their footsteps.

It means not following the dictates of society as to how you express your sexuality. If you are gay, then you have a right to be gay openly, and not spend your precious life-time hiding your sexuality for fear you will be rejected or castigated. If someone cannot accept you for what you are,- gay, heterosexual, transvestite, or whatever, then that is their problem, not yours!

It means doing what you love doing and doing what you love, regardless of how other people feel about it.

It means accepting all aspects of yourself, the less-than-perfect parts as well as the admirable parts.

It means accepting your insecurities and fears as being normal, and not seeing yourself as some sort of freak because of them. Everyone has insecurities and fears, some people are just better at hiding them than others! None of us is perfect! If we were, then we would have no reason to be here in this earth dimension in the first place! And anyway, who gets to decide what normal is? What is the criteria? What is the yard-stick?

It means speaking your truth as you yourself see appropriate, and not as someone tells you. Keeping quiet about something in order to keep the peace is not going to work in the long run, or saying what you think other people want to hear is not doing any good for anyone. You need to speak your truth!

It means opening to the totality of your being, accepting all of yourself as being just fine the way you are.

It means not beating yourself up when you feel you have got something wrong or made a mistake. There is no such thing as making a mistake. Everything is a learning experience.

It means thinking of all that you have in your life and being grateful for it all instead of wasting time thinking about what you do not have at this particular point in time.

It means focusing on ways to enjoy yourself. Life is meant to be fun, not all doom and gloom.

It means giving yourself peace over not trying to keep up with everyone else or setting yourself unrealistic targets which you know are unachievable.

It means loving yourself unconditionally, seeing yourself as the beautiful Spiritual being you really are, and spreading your bright light to other people.

It means knowing that you have a right to be here, and not letting anyone dictate to you how you should or should not live your life.

It means understanding the statement *'wherever you go, there you are!'* In other words, you cannot run away from yourself or hide from yourself. And as you see yourself, so others will see you.

It means knowing what you can change, and accepting what you cannot change.

It means accepting your inherent divine nature and your unlimited potentiality within the Oneness of the Great Universal God Energy.

It means accepting that you have the power within you to rise above any struggle and be the best you can be.

In the Gospel of Thomas we read:

"Yeshua said: / 'If those who guide you say: 'Look, / the Kingdom is in the sky, / then the birds are closer than you. / If they say: Look, /it is in the sea, / then the fish already know it. / The Kingdom is inside you, / and it is outside you. / When you know yourself, then you will be known, / and you will know that you are the child of the Living Father; / but if you do not know yourself, / you will live in vain / and you will be vanity.' " (Logion 3)

Meaning that to know yourself is the key to everything.

And:

"His disciples questioned him: / 'Should we fast? How should we pray? How should we give / alms? What rules of diet should we follow?' / Yeshua said: / 'Stop lying. / Do not do that which is against your love. / You are naked before heaven. / What you hide will be revealed, / whatever is veiled will be unveiled.' " (Logion 6)

Yeshua is teaching us here to be who you are, stop the pretense and stop feeding the separation between being and appearance.

"Yeshua said: / 'A human being is like a good fisherman / who casts his net into the sea. / When he pulls it out, he finds a multitude of little fish. / Among them there is one fine, large fish. / Without hesitation, he keeps it and throws all the small fish back into the sea.' " (Gospel of Thomas, Logion 8)

Small things don't matter. Self-knowledge is paramount. What good is it to know the nature of all the universes if we do not know ourselves and if we do not know *That through which all is known?*

"Yeshua said: / 'Grapes are not picked from themselves, / nor figs from thistles, / for they do not give fruit. / The good offer goodness / from the secret of their heart. / The perverse offer perversity / from the secret of their heart. / That which is expressed / is what overflows from the heart.' " (Gospel of Thomas, Logion 45)

This impoverished way of being, which Yeshua tells us is soul-less, is self-destructive. Look at the nature of the trees. There is nothing hidden or concealed within their spirit. Likewise, the actions and words of individuals reveal the secret of their heart, the nature of their spirit.

" Yeshua said: / 'Whoever cannot free themselves from their father and their / mother cannot be my disciple. / Whoever cannot free themselves from their brother and sister / and does not bear their cross as I do / is not worthy of me.' " (Gospel of Thomas Logion 55)

The only way to live is in being free from surrounding society with all its dictates, demands and social conditioning. That is the only way we can become who we truly are. Only then can we accept and face ourselves in our full dimensions.

"Yeshua said: / 'Those who know the All / yet do not know themselves / are deprived of everything.' " (Gospel of Thomas, Logion 67)

Vast knowledge without inner transformation is an illusion. It is mere show. Self-knowledge is the key to all.

So be yourself! You are a unique manifestation of the creative power, intelligence and magnificence of the Great Universal God Energy.

And it may not be at all easy! We all are victims of personality theft! Parents, teachers, society, all trying to mould you into what they think you should be.

Be true to yourself! And when you can live true to yourself, then you cannot be false to anyone else!

CHAPTER 13:

Taking back your power

We saw in a previous chapter that our Higher Self is us in our undiluted Divine Essence, remaining in the higher vibration energy level frequencies, as we journey through each life-time, a Spiritual being having a physical experience to advance our soul evolutionary process. And we saw how our Higher Self knows all the answers to all the questions we could ever ask.

And we saw too how our thoughts return to us multiplied. What we send out, we get back, multiplied. The Law of Greater Returns! That's one of the great Spiritual laws of the Universe, indisputable, inviolable, unquestionable!

So you have the power! You *are* the power!

What power? The power to determine your own life and control what happens to you. The power to control the thoughts you send out! Those thoughts that go out from you and manifest. But, unfortunately, we have given our power away to controlling institutions. And in doing so, we have enslaved ourselves, trapped ourselves in a prison of our own making. Our power is our strength! Our power is our freedom! Our power is our ticket to happiness and peace! And we have given it away!

Everything is within you! You are the *All*!

But we have been programmed to hand over our power to other external authorities who claim to be able to save us, who claim to be the intermediaries between us and God, and we cannot access God except going through them. Yes, we have been offered a very attractive package! Handing over our power to controlling religions, external forces, who promise us salvation if we join their club, pay our money, obey their rules, and they will get us into heaven when we die! A very attractive package indeed! Removing the responsibility from us to them, and in this world where we are all caught up in busy lives, we hand over our power. But what we are promised in return for our submission and allegiance cannot be delivered! No one has the power to deliver what controlling institutions promise!

You and you alone are responsible for your own soul evolution. When you arrive at the metaphorical pearly gates, blaming external forces who promised you this, promised you that, promised you a pass into heaven, holds no sway in the path your soul takes in the Spirit realms.

Your own heart, your own intuition guides you. Follow your heart, not your head or your mind. It is your head and your mind that have been taken over. It is your head and your mind that are being controlled by so many external forces. From you were a young child, you have been dictated to by all sorts of controlling regimes, told how to behave, how to think, what society expects of you, and it goes on all through your life. And we allow it all to happen! Simply because we have handed over our power!

And in handing over our power, we deny all responsibility for what happens. We blame others for our anger, our frustrations, depression, stress and unhappiness. But in terms of personal happiness, you cannot be peaceful while at the same time blaming others! When you stop blaming others, you will regain your sense of personal power.

No person can hurt you or offend you unless you allow them to do so. Meaning, it is not what is done to you that is important but how you react to what is done to you. And that is the part over which you have total control.

For example, you can react with road rage to another driver. That's your free choice. But you can also choose to defuse the situation and control the whole happening in another way. A way which produces positive results, instead of the negative road rage. You can dispel negative thoughts and feelings with positive productive thoughts and feelings. So instead of continuing in your anger, throwing out expletives and obscenities, simmering and smouldering with the smoke coming out your ears and nose, defuse the situation! Turn it around! Send that other driver thanks for giving you the opportunity to learn the lesson of patience and tolerance! And go quietly on your way!

Power and responsibility go hand in hand. Responsibility is automatically inherent in power. And we all have responsibility to use our power for the highest good of all. Many falsely hold on to the idea that escaping responsibility will produce freedom. They think that a holiday or time away will give them freedom. But wherever you go, there you are! You take everything with you! And upon return from such short-term escapades the same situation awaits you. And why? Because the world does not come *at* us, but *from* us! We create our own reality! We have that power!

So you and you alone are responsible for your own Spiritual evolution. You and you alone are responsible for every thought, every word, every action you send out on a particular energy vibration frequency! What you send out, you get back!

Be aware of your words and thoughts! Everything, absolutely everything originates in thought, and then becomes manifest. All the great works of art, all the great inventions down through history, all began in the mind, which is not the physical part of us. The room in which you are sitting, the clothes you are wearing, the tools and equipment you use every day are all the creative manifestation of many minds. Creative energy at work, coming from your thought process!

So everything is a projection of the mind! A projection of thought process! And you are in control of your thoughts!

When we understand life's experiences, we view responsibility differently. Love frees the mind and heart to respond generously to life's experiences, seeing in them all an opportunity to learn some valuable lesson. Unfortunately, few people know the secret of responsibility. Taught by elders the necessity of being responsible, often the purpose and meaning are lost and left unknown. People tend to value responsibility but view it as a trap and a burden of adulthood. In reality, it is our ability to respond to anyone, at any time, anywhere, that gives us freedom.

Daily we are bombarded with newspapers and media reports, and we very seldom question the source of such information fed to us. We fail to recognise that it is all government controlled, and the one view-point is being programmed into our belief system.

It is time for us all to stop blaming other people for what happens to us! We are in control of how we react!

Just change your thoughts, and you will change your words. Change your words and you will change your ways. Changing your ways will change your life. And changing your own life is the only way you can change the world.

In the Gospel of Thomas, Logion 48 we read:

"Yeshua said: / 'If two make peace with each other in a single house / then they can say to the mountain: 'Move!' / And it will move.' "

Meaning that before we can bring peace to the world or to others, we must be at peace with ourselves, we must make peace with all the various parts of ourselves. And when we are at peace with ourselves, through controlling our thoughts, then we can bring peace to the world.

And don't forget, of course: *'You always get in your life what you think about the most.'*

That's how powerful each and every one of us really is! The power to change the world through our thoughts! The power to manifest what we most desire through our thoughts!

It is time for us to take back our power. It is time for us to stop blaming other people for what happens to us. It is time for us to take responsibility for our own soul evolution. And it is time for us to accccept collective responsibility for how our governments and world leaders act! We voted them into power, and that means we must hold them accountable to us for their actions!

CHAPTER 14:

Non-judgement and Forgiveness

Non-judgement and forgiveness are synonymous. They go together, hand in hand, inherent in each other. And why? Simply because if you do not judge anyone, then there is no need for forgiveness, because in refusing to judge anyone, you have not created something which requires forgiveness.

Non-judgement and forgiveness are not an act. They are both an attitude. An attitude is a state of being. It is a thought system, a thought process. When we practise non-judgement and forgiveness often enough, they both become an automatic process, a way of life.

As we saw in an earlier chapter, our soul's sole mission in this incarnation here on this dense vibration energy level we call Planet Earth, is to evolve our immortal soul. And that means advancing our soul awareness, increasing our soul consciousness, upping our game to the stage where we identify each and every other person, including ourselves, as the pure Spiritual energy each and every one of us truly is, all connected and inherent in the Great Universal God Energy that encompasses absolutely everything that is, that ever has been and that ever will be. And, when we can get ourselves raised to that state of being, and see the bright Spiritual light each one of us is, a Spiritual being, pure and innocent, and not just a physical body, then we will not judge, we will not condemn, we will not kill.

Furthermore, we also saw earlier that we each come into this incarnation with our own agenda, our own blue-print for our own life-plan, a detailed plan for us to learn the certain lessons which we have freely chosen to learn. When we manifest in this vibration energy level, there is a veil of forgetfulness pulled down over our eyes, simply because if we remembered everything, then there would be no point in us coming here in the first place! And so we do not know what our own life-plan is, never mind the life-plan of anyone else, so how can we judge anyone else's actions? We cannot! We just do not know from where anyone else is coming or why they are here, what role they have agreed with us, at soul level, to play in our life, and so how can we feel that we are in a position to judge anyone?

And I explained earlier that God does not forgive, simply because there is nothing for God to forgive, as karma takes care of all that! We are not viewed from the Spirit energy dimensions as we are viewed here on Planet Earth. Judgement and forgiveness can only happen on the one level of existence, which is our dense vibrational level of existence here on Planet Earth. On a higher energy frequency of existence judgement and forgiveness do not exist. There is no need for either judgement or forgiveness where unconditional love is all that is known.

We exist on more than one level of existence. In the other levels of existence where we exist simultaneously, we do not look like we appear in this earth dimension, therefore those on the other levels of existence do not see us we are here on this earth plane, but as we are on the other higher dimensions, a bright Spiritual light, knowing only unconditional love. And it is the same with the spirit of our loved ones already passed over, they do not see us as we are here on this existence, on this energy vibration. So they do not see us picking our nose or performing any of our necessary bodily functions. That's a relief! They see us in our Spiritual form. As do the angels and all higher vibration frequency beings of Light. There is nothing to forgive! Forgiveness and judgement do not even appear on the radar! Judgement and forgiveness have no bearing or significance on an energy vibration level where unconditional love reigns supreme.

But here on this dense physical energy dimension of earth, the one single act we can perform which is guaranteed to bring us joy, inner peace and harmony is the act of forgiveness.

And why? Simply because when we forgive someone, we are releasing ourselves from carrying that weight of hatred, jealousy, resentment, whatever, around with us. We are freeing ourselves! Fact!

When you harbour feelings of envy, hatred, anger or whatever, towards any other person, then you are actually the one, and indeed the only one who is suffering, weighed down with destructive, debilitating negative energy. You are actually punishing and torturing yourself for the misdeed of someone else! Meanwhile, the person at whom your anger, hatred or resentment is directed, is sailing on peacefully, totally unaffected and totally unaware of how you are feeling! Yes, you are the only one suffering! And you are making yourself suffer! Unnecessarily!

And of course, we are all *One*. So next time you find yourself tempted to judge anyone, ask yourself, would I judge or accuse myself of this? The answer you receive from your Higher Self, your pure undiluted God Essence, will no doubt stop you in your tracks!

And remember! What we send out we get back, multiplied! When we fail to forgive, all we are doing is continuing to send out negative energy in the form of hatred or desire for revenge. We are just adding to the toxins already out there! The outcome will indeed be painful! OUCH!

And remember too! There is no judgement when it comes our time to pass back to the Spirit realms at the end of our physical life. No judgement whatsoever, in any way, shape or form!

And that most certainly must be a great consolation!

CHAPTER 15:
The Spiritual Laws of the Universe

The universe is self-regulatory, self-adjusting and self-replenishing. And there are laws governing all of this, powerful forces continuously active which affect and give order to our very existence. In just the same way as there are physical laws governing Planet Earth and all of Creation, such as the law of gravity; what you throw up in the air must come down again; the more heavy an object is, the faster it will fall, and the laws that keep the planets all revolving around in space without bumping into each other, so too there are what we call Spiritual laws and principles. These Spiritual laws and principles are the process through which that which was unmanifest now becomes that which is manifest.

It is these so-called Spiritual Laws of the Universe that keep the universe in balance, that keep the energy flowing as it is meant to flow. Otherwise, the energy would stagnate, like congealed blood, which blocks your arteries and prevents your blood flowing around your body as it is meant to flow, freely, and does so effortlessly, with no input from you.

It is adherence to these Spiritual laws of the universe that enable us to attain self-mastery, and it is adherence to these same Spiritual laws of the universe that enable us to live a life of joy and abundance. But we have never been taught about these laws at any stage in our education. And why have we never been taught about these laws? Because they are Spiritual laws. They are not the laws of religion, religion and Spirituality being two very different things. It is knowledge of these Spiritual laws of the universe that frees our soul to follow its own path and sing its own rapturous song, released from the shackles of controlling religions and dictatorial institutions.

In previous chapters, we have already considered some of these Spiritual laws, such as being true to yourself; non-judgement; forgiveness; karma; non-attachment; going with the flow; what you send out you get back; creating your own reality through your thoughts, and the universe as a mirror. But there is one very important Spiritual Law of the Universe which we have not yet considered. And that Spiritual Law is the law that governs the whole process of giving and receiving.

Giving and receiving is a two-way process. And like all such processes, there must be a balance. Everything must be in balance. Absolutely everything. The universe operates on a continuous basis of giving and receiving, the flow of energy always in dynamic cyclical movement.

Many people confuse receiving with taking. Receiving is NOT taking. Receiving is graciously accepting what others offer to us through kindness or in their desire to be of service. We often refuse their offers of kindness or help because we mistakenly feel we do not want to burden them, we do not want to put them out in any way, we do not want to bother or annoy them with our problems. Or indeed, because we feel that we, and we alone, can sort it! Too much independence is not a good thing! We saw earlier how we are all inter-dependent, inter-connected beings, and how nothing survives of its own accord, including us.

We have come here to this earth dimension to serve! To serve each other, and all humanity. That is part, the greatest part of our soul evolutionary programme! Our soul cries out to give. Giving is programmed into our very nature, into our very being, into our very fabric. Our right hand is our giving hand, our left hand our receiving hand. Giving and receiving is a cyclical movement. There are no straight lines or sharp ends in the Spiritual laws of the universe. Everything is in cyclical motion. What goes around, comes around. Everything must be kept in circulation. Money too must be kept in circulation, like everything else. Whatever you hoard, you lose.

So, if we all need to give, then we must all be equally willing to receive or accept from others. If no one is willing to accept, then that negates any form of giving, the very thing which we have come here to do! By refusing to accept or receive, what are we actually doing? By refusing the kindness of others, a helping hand, we are denying them the chance to advance their soul evolutionary process. That, surely, puts giving and receiving in a whole new light!

Whether it is something material, a compliment, an act of kindness, or a word of compassion, encouragement or praise, whatever, we all need to be willing to accept, and to show gratitude for that kindness. When we give from the heart, with unconditional love, and without seeking reward, return or even recognition, we immediately set in motion an unstoppable flow of energy that must, by the Spiritual laws of the universe, return to us multiplied. It does not need to be anything expensive or extravagant that we give, it is the intention that counts. And when we give with love, not expecting anything in return, then it is that intention that sets off the unstoppable chain of returning the same to us.

When you pay your bills, do so with gratitude to the universe for the service you have enjoyed, and for the fact that you have the money to pay those same bills. And when you pay with gratitude and not grudgingly, then you send out into the ether a positive energy which is going to bring more good things back to you. That's the Spiritual universal law!

It is better to give a little to a lot of people rather than a lot to just one person or to a select few. Why? Because giving to just one person or to a select few closes the circuit, curtails and limits the flow. The circuit must be kept open.

And we must be open to receive! We must be open to receive all the gifts that the universe is constantly sending us. And we must express gratitude for each and every gift. Why? Because again, that expression of gratitude immediately sets in motion another unstoppable surge of energy that returns more of the same to us!

Yes, giving and receiving in equal balance is one of the Spiritual laws of the universe. The fact that there is more taking in our present world and not enough of a balance between receiving and giving has left our present world in a serious state of imbalance.

And don't forget! You can only give out what you take in! Like your purse! No money in, then no money out! If you do not take in enough for yourself, then you are not in a position to give to anyone else or to be able to help them. You are the most important person in your life, and if you are not up to par, then you are no good to anyone else. So nurture yourself first and foremost, and that means allowing others to give to you in whatever way that may be.

CHAPTER 16:

We are not alone

Most people now accept that we here on Planet Earth are not the sole living organisms in a limitless and boundless cosmos. Anyone who tunes in regularly to Sky Television's discovery, history and science channels will no doubt be aware of the recently increased number of documentary programmes dealing with ancient civilizations, aliens, extra-terrestrials and various unexplained phenomena. Reputable and learned people are presenting us with very convincing material and evidence on a constant and on-going basis, material that must surely force us to re-think.

And who are these people who are pushing the boundaries of credibility for us? Forcing us to ask questions in search of the truth? These are not faceless people. They are very much up front about what they do, say and write. They hide behind no screens. They are unafraid to give us their findings and theories, unabashed about how they are indeed breaking the boundaries of science, history, archaeology and re-defining all things Spiritual and metaphysical.

Erich Anton Paul von Däniken is a Swiss author of several books which make claims about extraterrestrial influences on early human culture, including the best-selling *Chariots of the Gods'* published in 1968.

David Hatcher Childress is an American author, and the owner of Adventures Unlimited Press, a publishing house established in

1984 specializing in books on unusual topics such as ancient mysteries unexplained.

Giorgio A. Tsoukalos is a Greek historian, and host of the television series *'Ancient Aliens'*. He is a Swiss television personality and producer and a prominent proponent of the idea that ancient alien astronauts interacted with ancient humans.

Robert Bruce Clotworthy is an American actor and voice actor. Clotworthy is best known as the narrator for the History Channel series *'Ancient Aliens'* and his role as the voice of Jim Raynor in the StarCraft video.

Alan Butler is a writer, researcher, and recognized expert in ancient cosmology and astronomy with many books to his credit, including *'Hiram Key Revisited'*, *'Civilization One'*, and *'City of the Goddess'*. He has appeared on *'Ancient Aliens'*, *'The Mystery of History'*, and *'America Unearthed'*.

Andrew Collins is a science and history writer, and the author of books that challenge the way we perceive the past. They include *'From the Ashes of Angels'*, *'Gods of Eden'*, *'Gateway to Atlantis'*, *'Tutankhamun: The Exodus Conspiracy'* (co-authored with Chris Ogilvie Herald*)*, *'The Cygnus Mystery'*, *'Göbekli Tepe: Genesis of the Gods'* and *'The Cygnus Key: The Denisovan Legacy,'* and *'Göbekli Tepe and the Birth of Egypt'*.

These men are but a few of the many faces we see regularly on our television screens, presenting us with information that shows or at least strongly suggests that we are not alone in this universe.

We saw throughout this book how everything, including ourselves, is energy and how the only difference between all forms of life is the energy frequency level on which we all exist. As energy, we here on this dense earth energy frequency are vibrating at a level sustainable on this Planet Earth. We need food; we need water; we need air. Without these, we would not exist!

But! By that I merely mean we would not exist on this Planet Earth, in our present form. But we would still exist! As we saw in earlier chapters, there is no beginning and there is no end. We have always been in existence and we always will be in existence. We will always still exist in some other shape or form, in some other dimension, on some other energy vibration. We know there is life in different dimensions: the Spirit World; the Celestial Kingdoms; the Elemental Kingdoms. We know too that Earth is the planet with the most dense vibration; that is why it is such a desirable school for souls, affording greater opportunities to learn lessons that are not able to be learned in higher vibration dimensions. And why not? Simply because the lower based attributes such as greed, jealousy, self-ishness, ego, anger, do not exist on higher dimension levels of existence. We here on Planet Earth have the monopoly on all of these. Those souls in existence on other dimensions higher than that of Planet Earth operate only on Love, unconditional Love. That is all they know. They do not do war, violence, greed, hostility of any kind. They have progressed above that level. That is where we are heading too; but it will take some of us longer than others to get there, especially those of us still stuck in the lower third dimensions.

So of course we cannot expect to find life in any other part of the Galaxy similar to life here on Planet Earth. Conditions do not allow for it. Conditions are not right for life as we know it to be able to manifest. But other, higher vibrational forms of life do not need what we need here on earth in order to exist! In the Spirit world, there is no necessity for food; no necessity for water; no necessity for air. And why not? Because there are no human physical bodies there! Only our human physical bodies require all of those. As we progress up through the Spiritual ranks, we move to higher vibrational energy levels, and we continue in existence as a higher, lighter form of energy.

And those higher, lighter energy frequency vibration levels are not vacant, awaiting our arrival! They are full of other life-forms. These life-forms can see us, but we cannot see them; only when they allow us to see them! The raising of the earth's vibration in 2012 has made us more accessible to them. There are civilizations millions of light years ahead of us, but still all connected to us in the flow of the Great Universal Field of Energy.

We cannot ascend individually. We must ascend collectively. And here is where these recent programmes on television are so relevant. These programmes are all suggesting and pointing towards the theory that other life-forms are reaching out to us, to give us a helping hand up the ascension ladder, towards enlightenment. They are even strongly suggesting that ancient civilizations, such as ancient Greece, ancient Rome, the Mayan and Aztec Civilizations, to name but a few, were being helped by some sort of extra-terrestrial component. How else can we explain the amazing technological and architectural feats they accomplished? The building of the pyramids, for example? Feats that we today cannot accomplish!

These television documentaries are all showing the strong possibility that extra-terrestrial forces have been visiting us here on Planet Earth for centuries upon centuries, teaching us their skills in an effort to help us progress on our Spiritual path. They suggest that great minds such as Leonardo da Vinci in the Middle Ages were in some sort of communication or correspondence with extra-terrestrial beings. These extra-terrestrial beings who were instilling into da Vinci's mind the great inventions that he came up with. For example, his plans for a helicopter. Was there some greater, more advanced being from beyond our physical earth realm instructing him? And how about all the great people throughout history? Great leaders, great teachers, great prophets? Were they all in touch with some extra-terrestrial beings?

And what about U.F.O's? There are certainly more sightings of them now being reported. But what exactly are they? Could we in fact be seeing various versions of the Merkabah that we read about earlier? These U.F.O's are all reported to be like a spinning sphere, just like the Merkabah, which as we saw earlier is a protective vehicle of transport for our light body, our energy body, transporting us through the various energy frequency dimensions. Could these merkaba be light bodies from higher energy dimensions breaking through the ever-increasingly thinning veil between our earth dimension and the

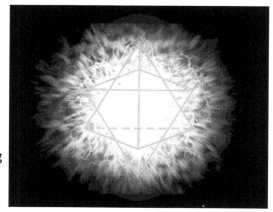

higher energy dimensions?

It certainly seems, from all accounts, that we are indeed surrounded on all sides by a vast array of other-dimensional beings, cosmic, planetary and solar hosts, all reaching out to us in the hope of offering us help. The true unity, inter-connectedness, inter-dependency and inter-relationship of everything cannot be over-emphasised. And the fact that we must all ascend collectively means that when these other-worldly beings help us, they are helping themselves!

And a final thought! Could there be extra-terrestrial beings walking amongst us now on Planet Earth?

Just keep an open mind! And an open eye! Nothing that we can imagine is impossible!

CHAPTER 17:

No beginning and no end

There has never been a time when you were not in existence. And there will never be a time when you will not be in existence. We are all energy, and energy never ceases to exist. It simply changes form.

"The disciples asked Yeshua: / 'Tell us, What will be our end?' / Yeshua answered: 'What do you know of the beginning, / so that you now seek the end? / Where the beginning is, the end will also be. / Blessed are those who abide in the beginning, / for they will know the end and will not taste death.' "   (Gospel of Thomas)

Everything is cyclical, and in a cycle, there is no beginning and there is no end. The end and the beginning are one and the same. Nothing is born and nothing dies. There is no birth, there is no death. Our true nature, our Divine Essence, is the nature of no birth and no death, no beginning and no end.

Nothing comes from nothing. Some-thing cannot be created from no-thing. And some-thing cannot be made into no-thing.

You did not come into being just when you left your mother's womb. Where did you exist before that? Before that you existed in the womb. Nor did you come into being at the moment of your conception. Where were you before that? Before that you were in both your parents. And before that? In your grandparents, and so on back to your earliest ancestors. And when you pass over to the higher vibration levels at the end of this life-time, that will not be

149

the end of you. You will live on in your children and in your grandchildren and all your descendants into infinity. That is why you have a responsibility to keep your physical body healthy and well. You are passing it on!

You have manifested out of the Great Universal God Energy, which has always been in existence. You are a unique manifestation of that Great Universal God Energy, and as such, you have always been within that Great Universal God Energy in some form or other. You do not appear out of nowhere or disappear into nowhere. You are always here, and you have always been here. You are just simply waiting for the correct conditions to present themselves in order for you to manifest yet again in another form.

There is no coming and there is no going. There is no place for us to come from, and there is no place for us to go to. We are always inherent within the Great Universal God Energy, we do not come or go from it, we are always in it, just manifesting under different guises. We do not come from anywhere and we are not going anywhere.

When conditions are sufficient and right, we manifest. That's it in a nutshell! We are not created, as being created suggests we were nothing before, and that we have now been made out of nothing. But nothing can come from nothing. Some-thing cannot come from no-thing.

Consider this. As sometimes happens, a baby in the womb does not go through the full pregnancy period. How can this be explained? What has happened is simply that the incoming soul sees that conditions are not right for it to manifest yet in this earth dimension. And so it withdraws. It does not go anywhere, but simply waits for the right conditions to materialise in order that it can manifest again.

Just like when you go into a dark room. How do you get rid of the darkness? By brushing it all up and putting it into a bin to be disposed of? Hardly! You get rid of the dark by turning on the light switch. The darkness has not gone anywhere, it is still there and will manifest again when conditions are right, specifically when you turn off the light. The darkness is there all the time, just waiting to manifest, just waiting for the right conditions to materialise to enable it to manifest.

The greatest fear that many people have about what they call '**death**' is that they will become nothing. That is because they see only the '**self**'. But the '**self**' does not exist. Nothing exists in and of itself. We are all a composite of something much bigger, but nevertheless a vital ingredient of that greater entity.

Nothing can ever exist by itself alone. Our very state of **being** entails of necessity **inter-being**. The flowers, the trees, the insects, the clouds, the rain, the sunshine, anything you care to mention, all **inter-be** with each other. Everything is dependent on everything else and everything is contained in everything else. For example, even the sheet of paper you hold in your hand. It has no independent **self**. Look at all the cosmic forces that came into play to allow that sheet of paper to manifest. The trees that provided the material, the soil that supported and nourished the trees, the sun that provided the light and the energy to grow the trees, the clouds that provided the rain to water the trees and enable them to grow, and so it goes on and on indefinitely. Everything **inter-is** with everything else. There is no state of *self*. There is no state of separate *being*. There is only the state of *inter-being*.

And within and inherent in this permanent state of *inter-being*, there is only impermanence, in the sense that everything, being energy, is constantly changing. Nothing, absolutely nothing stays the same, even for a few seconds in earth time.

Take the sheet of paper again. If you burn it, have you destroyed it? Have you ended its existence? No! What you have actually done is change its form. It is now ashes, but you have not annihilated it. How do you exterminate or make the ashes cease to be? You cannot! So you see, that sheet of paper has had no beginning, as it was always present in some form in the elements that go to manifest it. And it will manifest when the conditions come together that are necessary for it to manifest. Likewise, that sheet of paper will have no end, even if you reduce it to ashes, all you have done is change its format. It no longer exists as a sheet of paper, but it is still in existence in some other form, in this case, ashes.

Now consider this. If, as we have just seen, there is no beginning and there is no end, everything being in a permanent state of existence, just waiting to manifest as a particular object when the conditions come together, when the cosmic forces come together to enable it to manifest at that particular time, then everything we desire or need is already out there, in some state of existence. Just waiting to manifest! Just waiting to *be-come*!

And how do we manifest anything? We manifest through our thoughts! When we send our thoughts out there into the universe, cosmic forces instantly begin the process through which they will manifest. We are all familiar with the statement, **'be careful what you wish for, you might just get it!'** You definitely will! That's the Law of the Universe! You are just calling into action the cosmic forces necessary to enable your request to manifest. But nothing is being **created** or made! That object is simply manifesting because the conditions are now right for it to manifest! For it to **be-come**!

And here is another consideration. In this whole concept of there being no beginning and no end, only manifesting when conditions are right, there is no permanence, as everything is in a constant state of change, and it is this impermanence that we often have difficulty dealing with. We want things to stay the same. But things, by their very nature, do not stay the same.

Now let us push this a little further!

We have just seen that nothing stays the same. However, ironically, at the same time as there is nothing remaining the same, nothing becomes different.

Nothing is different and nothing stays the same. How do we explain this?

Well, think about when you paint your garden fence. You have just given it a new coat of paint. Is it different now? Is it the same? Yes to both questions! The fence is different in that it has been painted and freshened up, with a new look. But it is the same fence! The basic structure and fabric of the fence have not changed.

Or look at a photograph of yourself when you were much younger. Is that the same person you are now, or are you different? You certainly look different, as you have grown older, but it is still you. You are both different and the same.

Or consider the candle flame that you are about to light. You have the match, you have the candle. You strike the match, and the flame from the match lights the flame in the candle. But is the flame in the candle different from or the same as the flame from the match? Where does the flame from the match end and the flame from the candle begin? Where did the flame come from? Did you create it? No! You needed the match to enable the flame to manifest as a flame. It did not come out of *no-where* or materialise from *no-thing.* It was there all along, just waiting to manifest. Just waiting to *be-come*! When circumstances were right!

Get the analogy?

There is no beginning and there is no end. There is no coming and there is no going. There is no sameness and there is no difference.

And that's us! Just like everything else in this earth dimension! We have always been in existence and we always will be, in some form or other of energy. We are just waiting for the right conditions to come together to enable us to manifest in a particular form or shape at any particular time. We have not come from anywhere and we are not going anywhere. We are always here! We are not the same, in that we have changed form, but we are not different, as we are still the same basic energy.

And there is no *self.* There is only collective energy.

Energy is the building block of all that is. We are a manifestation of that energy, a consciousness, a consciousness which is constantly changing as we access the higher vibration energy frequencies, and always in existence.

There has been no beginning to us and there will be no end! We are cyclical, like cosmic re-cycled air-conditioning! Coming around again and again and again, throughout infinity and eternity, always present, just manifesting in different energy forms when cosmic conditions are right and in place to enable us to manifest.

No beginning and no end!

CONCLUSION
Spiritual Awareness and Enlightenment

We are all Christs in the making, all destined for Christhood. And by that I mean we are all destined to achieve *Spiritual Awareness* and attain *Spiritual Enlightenment.*

So what is the difference between achieving *Spiritual Awareness* and attaining *Spiritual Enlightenment*? We are not taught anything about any of this in school. This has nothing to do with books, degrees or anything our education systems instil into us. Nor do we learn about any of this through religious channels. And why not? Simply because this is all about our Spiritual path, our Spiritual journey, as individual and unique for each one of as is our individual and unique physical body.

The word *Spiritual* is common to both. That's a key to our understanding. *Spiritual Awareness* happens in this life-time, *Spiritual Enlightenment* happens beyond this earth energy vibration. You can awaken in this energy dimension, you can achieve *Spiritual Awareness* while here on earth in this life-time but you cannot usually achieve *Spiritual Enlightenment*. In fact, it is on this earth energy vibration that we *must* achieve *Spiritual Awareness*. That is the reason why we are here! And that is the reason why we will keep coming back time and time again, until we do manage to achieve *Spiritual Awareness*. Achieving *Spiritual Awareness* is what gets us off the wheel of re-incarnation, ending the cycle of us having to return again and again. And when we pass on after each life-time, the one and only criteria which registers with our soul is the particular stage we are at in gaining **Spiritual Awareness**. Our soul automatically gravitates towards the level in the Spirit world which we have gained for ourselves through our **Spiritual Awareness**.

Achieving **Spiritual Awareness** is not heralded by trumpet blasts, fireworks or thunder and lightning. Nor is it ushered in by any remarkable occurrence such as that which Paul was reported to have experienced on his way to Damascus!

Achieving **Spiritual Awareness** is nothing more than an awakening, a realization, an awakening to a clear seeing of all that we are not, and a direct realization of what we truly are. It is a clear understanding, a clear knowing and an undoubted accepting that we are one thing appearing as everything.

Achieving **Spiritual Awareness** or awakening involves the realization that I am the **All**, I am the **One**.

Achieving **Spiritual Awareness** is knowing that we are all part of a unified field of energy, from which we have manifested, from which we derive our very being, and to which we are inseparably and eternally connected. Scientists call this the Zero Point Field. Religions apply the various terms of the Tao; Nirvana; Kingdom of Heaven. Most of us simply call it God.

And the good news is, you do not have to become a hermit, living in the desert existing on insects and wild honey, or on a remote mountain somewhere in order to achieve **Spiritual Awareness**. In fact you do not have to give up worldly things at all! Or even deny yourself physical comforts. The physical body is part of our experience in this physical world. We are living here for a purpose, so we need to be in this dimension, but we do not need to immerse ourselves completely in it! We are *in* this world but we are *not of* it!

Achieving *Spiritual Awareness* or awakening will not come from reading sacred texts. *Spiritual Awareness* or awakening is not something someone else can give you. It will only come from within you. And no-one can awaken you. You can only awaken yourself, when you are ready. Each person needs to open his own eyes, and not try to see through the eyes of anyone else. Teachers, sages and prophets can all bring us to the door, but we must go through on our own.

Inner peace is the only way to achieve *Spiritual Awareness*. And the tool to gain inner peace is meditation. Spiritual awakening happens when we stop battling against our natural self, and when we stop berating ourselves for not being good enough.

And the other good news? Merely having the desire for achieving *Spiritual Awareness* is enough to begin the process. All we have to do is listen to life all around us! All we have to do is see the hand of the creative energy of God in everything, and God personified in everyone we meet.

With achieving *Spiritual Awareness* or awakening, we stop controlling, we stop chasing after things, we cease wanting and we begin to realize that all is well, because all is now indeed well within our being. And as within, so without! When we are at peace in our own inner world, at peace in our own being, then the outer world around us reflects that, and so is agreeable for us too. We have a clear perception of the world, seeing the problems of war, violence, poverty and suffering without using them as an excuse to get all worried and worked up.

Spiritual Awareness is not achieved through doom and gloom. We will never raise our Spiritual Consciousness through doom and gloom! Doom and gloom only brings us suffocation, entrapment, slavery. Slavery to what? Slavery to controlling religions who preach doom and gloom, forever parading before us the images of a dying Jesus on the cross, in order to control us through the double-edged sword of fear and guilt. Religious philosophies and beliefs have nothing to do with *Spiritual Awareness* or *Spiritual Awakening.* Achieving *Spiritual Awareness* does not require any special prayers, incantations, spells or whatever. It is about gaining true freedom and realizing experientially what and who we truly are.

Achieving *Spiritual Awareness* liberates us from fear and anxiety, simply because fear and anxiety are both nothing but thought, an idea, a notion, and in the process of achieving *Spiritual Awareness*, we are moving beyond such thought. Achieving Spiritual Awareness sets us free, liberates us. Being in the state of *Spiritual Awareness* is *being* free!

Achieving *Spiritual Awareness* means being able to live in and being fully focused on the present moment. Being fully focused on the present moment means we do not worry or fret, but expand our consciousness to experience all that we are and All That Is. We have no troubled past with which to contend, as there is no past! This present moment is the only moment there is, the only moment where life in all its fulness takes place.

Whilst achieving *Spiritual Awareness* or awakening is belonging to this world, attaining *Spiritual Enlightenment*, on the other hand, is not of this world. It exists beyond physicality.

Jesus the Master came to this earth dimension to show us how we can achieve *Spiritual Enlightenment*, how to get off the wheel of re-incarnation, how to attain Christ Consciousness. Because yes, that is what *Spiritual Enlightenment* is! It is Christ Consciousness! The highest level of consciousness, the highest level of energy within the whole hierarchical structure of the Great Universal God Energy.

Attaining *Spiritual Enlightenment*, just like achieving *Spiritual Awareness*, is not heralded by trumpet blasts or fire works. And again, like achieving *Spiritual Awareness*, attaining *Spiritual Enlightenment* has nothing to do with gathering knowledge or reading as many Spiritual books as you can get your hands on. Teachers telling you to take firm control of your life, achieve this goal, achieve that goal, and so on. Have a plan! Yes, we have all seemingly just got to have a plan! '*If you fail to plan, you plan to fail*' we are often told.

But look at Buddha! Did Buddha have a plan? A plan to do what? The only plan Buddha had was to laugh and *just be*! Plans will not help us to either achieve *Spiritual Awareness* or attain *Spiritual Enlightenment*.

Spiritual Enlightenment, or Ascension as it is also termed, means simply raising our energy vibration, increasing our energy vibration to the highest level, the level at which we become pure Light. It is the end of the process that began as achieving *Spiritual*

Awareness.

Attaining **Spiritual Enlightenment** means that we now live in a perpetual state of pure thought, joy and freedom. We are now in the ranks of the Ascended Masters, radiating nothing but pure Light and unconditional Love, and from our highest vantage point, dedicated to helping the rest of humanity achieve **Spiritual Awareness** and attain **Spiritual Enlightenment.** Many people who attain **Spiritual Enlightenment** now choose to remain on this earth vibration and serve mankind on this frequency. These people, who choose to remain in their physical body, radiate at a higher vibration than the rest of us, and are noticeable by the glow that encompasses them and radiates from within them. Many Ascended Masters and Enlightened beings are walking amongst us now on this earth plane, serving to speed up the **Spiritual Enlightenme**nt process for all humanity. Many of these highly evolved beings have had experiences on other planets, in other galaxies and in other universes, and have now chosen to re-incarnate here in order to serve humanity once again in these exceptional times in which we are now living.

Being in the state of **Spiritual Enlightenment** means we have completed successfully all the missions we set ourselves through all our life-time after life-time of re-incarnation and we have balanced all our karmic debt. We are now in the **Spiritual Enlightenment** state where manifestation is instant, bi-locating and teleporting are simple and easy, and our powers are incredible, way beyond what we can even imagine on this earth plane, far beyond our limited perception as physical beings.

Plato summed it all up for us:

'I do nothing but go about persuading you all, old and young alike, not to take thought for your persons or your properties, but first to chiefly to care about the greatest improvement of the soul. I tell you that virtue does not come from money but that from virtue comes money and every other good of man, public as well as private.'

And in the Gospel of Thomas we read:

"His disciples asked: / 'Teach us about the place where you dwell, / for we must seek it.' / He told them: / 'Those who have ears, let them hear! / There is a light within people of light, / and they shine it upon the whole world. / If they do not shine it, / what darkness!'" (Gospel of Thomas Logion 24)

It cannot be made any more clear! The place where Yeshua dwells is the Light. Light fills all space and is invisible in itself, yet allows all things to be seen. To be in the Light is to have attained **Spiritual Enlightenment**.

Those who have achieved **Spiritual Awareness,** which is the first vital step on the path to **Spiritual Enlightenment,** are those who accept that every situation ***just is***. Those in the third dimension, which is this dense earth dimension, react to every situation with anger, aggression, impatience, or with some other negative energetic response, living by human laws. The **Spiritually Aware**, on the other hand, live by the Spiritual laws, free of worry or concern, secure in the knowledge that every thought, emotion, word or action operates on an energy vibration frequency which attracts similar events, situations and people on the same waveband.

As each one of us awakens and begins our path of **Spiritual Awareness**, we carry a light, a beacon, which shines out to everyone we meet. We will not transform the world by some mass collective movement or revolution. The world will only be transformed by turning on one light at a time, by spreading the flame from one person to the next, and the next and so on.

So let your light shine! Let your own sparkling light shine out to everyone you meet, as we all travel along the same path of **Spiritual Awareness** and to **Spiritual Enlightenment**! For that is the way we are all heading, every precious soul will eventually arrive back in the Light. No soul will be lost or forgotten, but it is up to each one of us to become awakened and to begin our own Spiritual journey.

As Silver Birch, the Native American Indian teacher told us:

'Until the soul is quickened and is aware of the higher, deeper, nobler and greater things of life, the individual is living in a mist.'

Eileen McCourt

Other Books by Eileen McCourt

Eileen has written sixteen other books, all of which are available on Amazon as either print copies or Kindle. For more information, visit her author page: www.eileenmccourt.co.uk

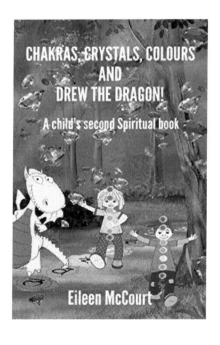

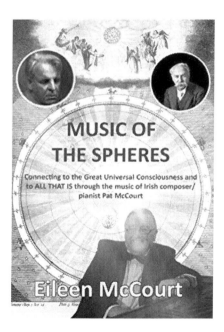

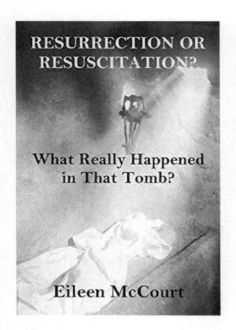

RESURRECTION OR
RESUSCITATION?

What Really Happened
in That Tomb?

Eileen McCourt

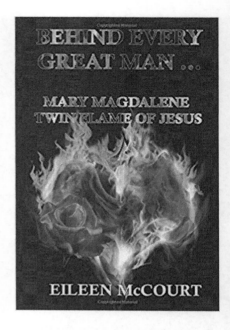

BEHIND EVERY
GREAT MAN ...

MARY MAGDALENE
TWIN FLAME OF JESUS

EILEEN McCOURT

DIVINELY
DESIGNED

THE ONENESS
OF THE TOTALITY
OF ALL THAT IS

Eileen McCourt

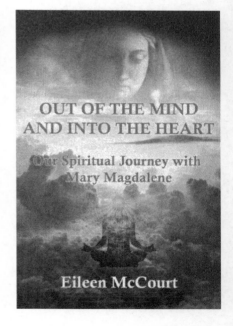

OUT OF THE MIND
AND INTO THE HEART

Our Spiritual Journey with
Mary Magdalene

Eileen McCourt

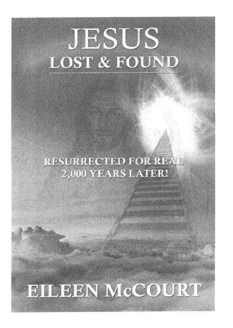

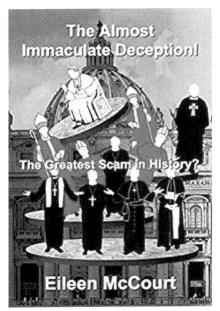

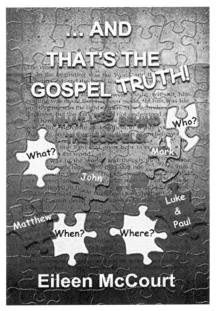

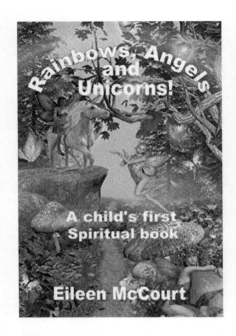

Rainbows, Angels and Unicorns!

A child's first Spiritual book

Eileen McCourt

LIFE'S BUT A GAME!

GO WITH THE FLOW!

A Spiritual Manual for Today's Teenagers & Young Adults

Eileen McCourt

SPIRIT CALLING!

ARE YOU LISTENING?

Eileen McCourt

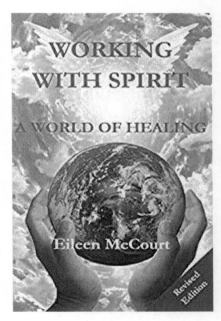

WORKING WITH SPIRIT

A WORLD OF HEALING

Eileen McCourt

Revised Edition

This Great
Awakening

The part we all play
in this time of our lives

Eileen McCourt

Living the Magic

Connecting the physical and
spiritual worlds

Eileen McCourt

Printed in Poland
by Amazon Fulfillment
Poland Sp. z o.o., Wrocław